This is a fantastic book by a great Christian leader. Powerful insights into the life of Peter will warm your heart, challenge your soul and fix your eyes on Jesus. Essential reading for every Christian who wants to grow. I loved it!
Wallace Benn, Bishop of Lewes.

Ken Clarke is a man worth listening to, and he speaks as he writes, from the heart to the heart. There is some rich wisdom in these pages as he looks at lessons from the life of Peter that apply to followers of Jesus in every generation. If you have been called to lead (or suspect you might be), there is much here to encourage you to grow and deepen your faith.
Ian Coffey, Vice-Principal (Strategy) and Director of Leadership Training, Moorlands College

Peter is by any standards an ordinary guy, but Jesus has a habit of taking the ordinary and hooking an extra on to it, and he can do the same for you.

My friend Ken 'Fanta' Clarke invites us to look at our own misgivings and uncertainties and, through the life of Peter, encourages, challenges and reminds us that God is not finished with us yet. Fanta candidly describes grappling with his own personal challenges, and shows that through prayer and action we can celebrate the wonderful gift of life afresh.

This book is not only an excellent resource in personal discipleship, but it is in every sense an enjoyable read that has deepened my faith and intimacy with God. The Emerald Isle has rolled out some fantastic orators and writers from its shores down through the years, and Fanta is up there with the best of them.
Keith Mitchell (Mitch), Evangelist with Crown Jesus Ministries and Author of Snatched From the Fire *(IVP)*

Going for
Growth

Going for
Growth

Learning from Peter

Ken Clarke

INTER-VARSITY PRESS
Norton Street, Nottingham NG7 3HR, England
Email: ivp@ivpbooks.com
Website: www.ivpbooks.com

First published 2011
Reprinted 2014

British Library Cataloguing in Publication Data
A catalogue record for this book is available from the British Library.

ISBN: 978–1–84474–546–3

Set in Dante 12/15pt
Typeset in Great Britain by CRB Associates, Potterhanworth, Lincolnshire
Printed and bound in Great Britain by Ashford Colour Press Ltd, Gosport, Hampshire

Inter-Varsity Press publishes Christian books that are true to the Bible and that communicate the gospel, develop discipleship and strengthen the church for its mission in the world.

Inter-Varsity Press is closely linked with the Universities and Colleges Christian Fellowship, a student movement connecting Christian Unions in universities and colleges throughout Great Britain, and a member movement of the International Fellowship of Evangelical Students. Website: www.uccf.org.uk

Contents

Foreword

I am delighted and very thankful to be invited formally to introduce Ken Clarke's wonderful book, *Going for Growth*. This writing comes from the 'pen' of a man who has been a special friend to me for many years. Together we have walked the beaches of Donegal, participated in conferences where the Bible was preached, and shared spiritual encouragement during times when one or both of us was experiencing exhilarating achievement or . . . (let's be honest) deep disappointment. Accompanied by our wives, Helen and Gail, we have travelled Ireland and parts of the United States, introducing one another to some of our favourite places.

I know Ken the husband and father, I've experienced Ken the natural humorist and deep thinker, and I'm familiar with Ken the pastor and bishop. I'm aware of his powerful influence in the Irish Christian community, and I am acquainted with Ken the missionary who has a heart for the world. Now I am getting to know Ken the writer.

This is a lot to know about a man, and I am the richer for it all. It causes me to say that, in all these dimensions of Ken Clarke's life, there is the consistent evidence of the beautiful Spirit of Jesus in all that he is and does.

Ken Clarke and I have long shared a mutual affection for Simon Peter. We have both been drawn to this premier disciple of the Lord because of his story, which tells of a journey from spiritual crudeness to sainthood.

In his early days of following the Lord, Simon Peter (presumptuous, loud-mouthed, egoistic) was the epitome of immaturity. In his latter days, Peter became a champion of compassion, creative leadership, and a passion to proclaim the redeeming Word of Jesus. Both Ken and I would like to think that, like Peter, we've grown a bit (at least a little bit) in these areas ourselves. *Going for Growth* offers insight into how that happens.

Ken's book, in my opinion, is best read in small chunks, perhaps a chapter a day during one's personal meditations. The author has thoughtfully described Simon Peter's life and growth as it was influenced by Jesus. He's offered it to us in a way that we can absorb, brood upon, and appropriate for our daily lives. Also, *Going for Growth* could be a marvellous book for a small group to read together. I can just imagine the depth and energy of dialogue when a group ties into Ken's insights.

What's so good about *Going for Growth* is that Ken Clarke has made Simon Peter believable. One reads each chapter and says, 'I think I could be this man. I understand his faults and flaws; I connect with his dreams and hopes. With God's help, I can emulate him.'

And that is why this book is such a pleasure to introduce and commend to you. You will find yourself meeting both Peter and his Lord in a fresh new way. And, as the title suggests, you will grow as a result (as I have).

Gordon MacDonald
Concord, New Hampshire
May 2011

Introduction

We all meet people in life who make an enormous impact upon us. We can identify with them. We see something of ourselves in them and we also see what we aspire to be. They influence us. They challenge us. They motivate and inspire us. They are people of hope. They show us a better way. They are like rainbows in human form, for they are pictures of potential realized and compelling transformation. In my life, the Apostle Peter is one such person. For years he has intrigued me and enthused me. I see in him a model for twenty-first-century disciples and leaders.

Growth is one of the buzzwords in the church today. Growing churches, growing leaders and growing Christians are familiar terms. Yet real sustainable growth is impossible without growth in integrity and Christ-likeness. This is a growth which is not about celebrity but about depth of character. It is about the kind of people we are and can become. This book is all about observing that kind of quality growth in Peter. It is about learning vital lessons from him.

Peter's story is a reality check to those who make false promises of a trouble-free life for all who follow Jesus. His life dispels a superficial and shallow understanding of Christian discipleship. His experiences are a reminder that growth involves growing pains. He knew about disappointment and unwise choices. He tasted the bitter pain of personal failure and foolishness. We see that failure does not have to be final and that brokenness can be the springboard to usefulness. Out of the seedbeds of deep devastation, we witness Christ-initiated restoration and Peter's incredible transformation. His story is one of hope for all, not least for those who feel a failure. The church today needs to rediscover a Christ who restores, and needs to be more like him.

However, Peter's story is much more than that. It goes far beyond the personal. The Peter story brings hope to divided communities and struggling churches. In Peter we see someone compelled to confront prejudices in his own life. Issues of racism, sectarianism and religious bigotry are part of his story. Having grown up in a divided community in Northern Ireland, and conscious of divisions in countries and communities across the world, I find Peter a model for courageous Christian leadership in our twenty-first-century world. He is compellingly contemporary. His experience gives hope to all.

This book has been a long time in the making. Sometimes I have said that preparing a sermon is comparable to a pregnancy, but writing this book has been even more like a pregnancy. I freely acknowledge that only a man would say that – more specifically, a man who is willing for martyrdom! However, the comparisons are that it doesn't happen instantly, it takes time, pain is involved and one changes during the experience. The delivery of this book is after a very long 'pregnancy'! Its conception was in 2002. I had the privilege of giving the Bible readings at an International Scripture Union Conference in Nottingham University. Some of this material has grown out of those Bible readings on Peter. New Horizon

is the largest annual Christian event in Northern Ireland
and completely unexpectedly in 2007, because of sudden
bereavement in a speaker's family, I was drafted in and led
Bible readings on Peter. At both events, people encouraged
me to consider publication. Some of these themes were
explored when the Bishops of the Church of Ireland invited
me to give a short series of devotional talks at one of our
residential meetings. Their subsequent comments were a
great encouragement.

I have been surrounded by a great company of people who
have urged me on to the birth of the book and to each one I
say a sincere thank you. Helen, my wife, and our four
daughters Alison, Tanya, Lynda and Nicola and their families
have been cheerleaders. Thank you also to friends overseas
who gave us hospitality during my sabbatical. Writing has
taken place in the homes of Bishop Derek and Alice Eaton
in Nelson, New Zealand, and Bishop Mark and Alison
Lawrence in Charleston, South Carolina. More work was
accomplished in the Christ The King Retreat Centre in Albany
Diocese, USA, thanks to the generosity of Bishop Bill Love
and his wife Karen. Gordon MacDonald will never know the
depth of influence he has had on my life, and I am grateful
to him for being so willing to write the foreword. To him and
his remarkable wife Gail, thank you for being to Helen
and myself an 'Aquila and Priscilla'.

When I married Helen I entered a tribe, the most amazing
family who have been one of God's greatest gifts in my life.
They have loved me generously and at times we have laughed
helplessly. To each one of the Goods I say thank you. IVP are
my first experience of publishers and they have been my best
experience! Kate Byrom has been an excellent editor and
through an unexpected teatime conversation with Ian Coffey
in Isaac's Hotel, Dublin, this book took its first breath.

My one prayer is that through reading *Going for Growth*, we will hear the voice of God speaking into our lives and go deeper with the Lord who loves us as much as he loved Peter. Like Peter may we 'grow in the grace and knowledge of our Lord and Saviour Jesus Christ' (2 Peter 3:18).

Ken Clarke
May 2011

Potential

When God looks at me,
what does he see?

1. The double vision of Jesus

'My parents have been the major influence on my Christian life.' This was the reply I received some years ago when I was interviewing several people for a post as Curate in our parish. I cannot think of any Christian parent who wouldn't be thankful to the Lord if one of their children said the same.

We are all influenced by others. As you think about your own life, who have been the strongest and most powerful influences? Perhaps your experience of parenting was quite different from my curate and so it may have been another member of the family, a friend, a school teacher or a work colleague who had the strongest and most powerful influence. Perhaps it was someone at an Alpha or Christianity Explored course, a youth worker, a pastor, a teacher in Sunday school, a Scripture Union worker or leader?

Pause

Take a few moments to reflect and thank the Lord for those who have influenced you positively in your Christian lives. Consider specifically how they helped or inspired you.

Peter was one of the inner core of disciples who had the privilege of being with Jesus, not only during Christ's three years of public ministry but at several pivotal points in his life. As we will see, Peter was present during the transfiguration experience. Later in his life he was with Jesus in the Garden of Gethsemane. He was one of the few disciples who continued to follow Jesus after his arrest in the Garden. Peter, with James and John, formed the inner circle. If we were to ask Peter who had most influenced his life, without any hesitation he would surely say, 'Jesus Christ.' Peter's preaching and teaching were utterly focused on Jesus. Peter proclaimed that 'there is no other name under heaven given to mankind by which we must be saved' (Acts 4:12). When the Lord was using him in healing, he declared, 'In the name of Jesus Christ of Nazareth, walk!' (Acts 3:6). In his epistles he wrote about Christ. Jesus Christ was the single most important person, and the greatest most powerful influence, in Peter's life.

However, although Peter was there at so many of the crucial points in the life of Christ, his presence was not always helpful. At times he was an embarrassment to himself, his Lord and others. In the pages of the Bible we see Peter the encourager and loyal follower. We see Peter the abysmal failure. We see Peter the disciple who was a dramatic disappointment. But how did his journey with Jesus begin?

It all started with a look . . .

Andrew, Simon Peter's brother, was one of the two who heard what John had said and who had followed Jesus. The first thing Andrew did was to find his brother Simon and tell him, 'We have found the Messiah' (that is, the Christ). And he brought him to Jesus. Jesus looked at him and said, 'You are Simon son of John. You will be called Cephas' (which, when translated, is Peter).

(John 1:40–42)

We can learn so much from how someone looks at us. Have you ever been introduced to someone and they have not even looked at you, let alone engaged with you? His or her eyes are staring at someone else across the room or the hall. The person says, 'I'm pleased to meet you,' but their body language – or more precisely, their eye language – is conveying the opposite message.

There can be so much in a look. Husbands and wives know only too well that look from a spouse which conveys a powerful message. Not one word is spoken but a great deal has been communicated. I remember attending a wedding reception where the father of the groom, in his post-dinner speech, made this controversial claim: 'When God invented women, he invented the look!' No doubt the groom's mother would have shared the same insight about men! Whatever the origin, it is undoubtedly true that there can be so much in a look.

Jesus looked at Peter. I wonder what Jesus was thinking as he did so. Was he thinking, 'I'm going to have some challenge with you!'? Many youth leaders have had the experience of surveying a group of young people gathered to set off on a holiday or activity, and immediately they can discern the person who will push everyone to their limits. There is always one at every youth camp! It is the same in many churches. As leaders we look at them for the first time and we think to ourselves, 'This one is going to be a stretch.' (Or perhaps it's another leader we are looking at!) Is that the kind of response Jesus has as he meets Simon?

You are . . . you will be

I think we have a hint of how Jesus was thinking from the words he spoke. 'You *are* Simon son of John, you *will be* called Cephas (which, when translated, is Peter).' The Methodist preacher, Dr Sangster, preached a sermon on these words, entitled 'The Double Vision of Jesus'. Jesus says, 'You are, but you will be.' Jesus sees double. He sees this man not only as he is at this precise moment, but also as what he can be and will be. He sees what he will become. That is how Jesus sees everyone. He looks at us and sees us not just as we are now, but as what we can become in him and through him. One preacher speaking on the life of Peter called his sermon 'The Pebble who became a Rock'. That is exactly what happened. Many people would not have shown any interest in this rough, tough, uncouth and unpredictable fisherman, but Jesus saw potential.

Jesus sees a person's value

Jesus sees potential in people whom others would write off. He values each and every person. He did not dismiss an ordinary person like Simon Peter. Others would have. No matter how Peter felt about himself, Jesus loved him and saw what he could be. With Jesus, each person is of immense value. His love is for all. His death was for the whole world. His hands reach out to every hand. His heart connects with each human heart.

The power of one

In a culture, even within the church, which can be preoccupied with big numbers, we need to recapture this Jesus vision of seeing the potential and the value of *one*. In Northern Ireland, and the wider UK, we have seen a growing disillusionment with politics and politicians. During one general election in the Republic of Ireland, I remember seeing car stickers which read: 'Don't vote, it will only encourage them!' The disillusionment is reflected in a low turnout at elections. Why? Part of the reason is because people feel that their vote doesn't matter. However, I wonder if the real reason is that people feel *they* don't matter. They have decided that one person can't make a difference. The Christian gospel disagrees. The gospel never underestimates the power of one, because Jesus doesn't.

One person does matter! In the stories of Jesus, the one lost sheep mattered to the shepherd. The one lost coin mattered to the owner. The one son who was lost still mattered to the father. One matters. One vote gave Oliver Cromwell control of England. One vote gave America the English language rather than German. One vote gave Adolf Hitler control of the Nazi Party. Never underestimate the power of one. The kingdom of God grows one by one. That young boy we meet, that girl in our school, that man who lives across the road, that woman who works in the same office, that young person who comes along for the first time to an event we have organized, that old person who no-one ever seems to visit. Each person matters to Jesus Christ.

One life filled with Christ's life *can* make a difference. *One* life filled with the awesome power of the Holy Spirit can make a huge impact. Simon Peter, one man, an uncouth fisherman, was used by Christ to change the course of this world's history. Esther, one woman with one voice, but surrendered to God, saved an entire nation (her story is told in the Book of Esther in the Old Testament). Boris Pasternak, the Russian poet, wrote, 'It is not revolutions and upheavals that clear the road to new and better days, but someone's soul inspired and ablaze.'

The man Simon Peter met inspired his soul. Peter's life and faith were set on fire by this woodworker from Nazareth. Jesus looked at him and saw him not only as he was. He looked with

his double vision and he saw what Simon could become . . .
one of the greatest Christian leaders the world has ever seen.

Jesus takes us and he makes us

Why is this message so important at this time? Because many
people today feel they are of no worth and that they have no
worth. They feel that they don't matter to anybody. They are
just a statistic or a number. They feel second class and of no
value to anyone. Like a currency, they are devalued at the
whims of others. They have the mindset of a reject. Perhaps
that is how you are thinking. Does that describe how you feel
about yourself? Isn't it extraordinary that in so many societies
today, individualism is rampant and yet individuals feel
worthless, useless, undervalued and devalued?

Life is full of surprises. In my own life I can certainly verify
the truth of that statement. The expected failed to materialize
. . . the unexpected unfolded and startled me. In preparing the
material for this book, and in reading about Peter in the New
Testament, I made an extraordinary discovery. Although I was
looking at Peter's life and actions, actually I was learning so
much more about Jesus. I have been impacted by the vision,
compassion, patience and love of Jesus for a loser. His encouragement is incredible. His model of teaching is impeccable.
Jesus brings out the potential in Peter. He trains him, prays
for him, helps him get up and get going again. Looking at
Peter means we are looking at what Jesus can do in the life
of an ordinary unpolished person, a rough diamond. It is
impressive, exciting and inspiring. We look at Peter. We marvel
at Jesus. That is the way Peter would have wanted it to be.
His passion, like that of John the Baptist, was to point people
to Jesus.

How many of us are where we are because someone saw
potential in us? They did not write us off as others might have

done. They prayed for us, encouraged us and were patient with us. They didn't give up on us. I remember at a Scripture Union weekend, when I was about fourteen years old, one of my school teachers was required to discipline me . . . and rightly so! It was the middle of the night and I had behaved so badly. I deserved it! He could have written me off for my selfish behaviour. But he didn't. He never gave up on me. To this day he keeps in touch.

The Scripture Union leader who led me to Christ in 1961 still prays for me every week. I receive a Christmas card from him every Christmas and he will write on it, 'Praying for you.' I know he means it. He really is praying for me, every single week since I was twelve years old. I can think of several people who have been praying for me for fifty years. I am so thankful for them. They are a reflection of the Lord who sees potential in each person and longs to see that potential fulfilled. Whoever we are, wherever we are, whatever age we are, Jesus sees potential in us. He has set his sights on us. He calls us to follow. He has promised to be with us. He gives us gifts. He looks at us with his double vision and sees what we can become.

Pushy, self-confident and brash

Peter was not the shy, quiet type. His fiery temperament was quite obvious and he couldn't disguise it. There was little that was subtle or nuanced about this fisherman. He wore his feelings on his sleeve. His tongue was overactive. His claims were non-productive. He was tactless and lacked self-control. With Peter there were no back doors. He just spoke out, gave out and, on occasions, lashed out! As a consequence there was often fallout from his words and actions.

If we were choosing a scene from nature to illustrate Peter's temperament and personality, it would be a massive volcano rather than a tranquil, wave-less lake. And the volcano is not an extinct one! Peter's personality was pushy, self-confident and brash. He was impulsive and explosive. He was hot-tempered in his attitude to other people and situations. He was undisciplined and acted on impulse rather than reason. He had a hot head and cold feet. He would speak now and think later, as his mind and his mouth did not always engage with one another.

In John 13, Jesus seeks to prepare his disciples for his departure. Peter asks the Lord where he is going and, having been told that he cannot follow now:

> Peter asked, 'Lord, why can't I follow you now? I will lay down my life for you.'
>
> Then Jesus answered, 'Will you really lay down your life for me? Very truly I tell you, before the rooster crows, you will disown me three times!'
> (John 13:37–38)

Jesus was absolutely right – Peter was way off the mark. This is typical Peter, making extravagant claims, rash promises and hasty responses. When the rubber hit the road, he denied the Lord, just as Jesus predicted, and once again his mouth and his intention rushed ahead of his foolish actions.

The volcano erupts

Let us take another example: the Garden of Gethsemane where Jesus was arrested. The circumstances are important. John 18 describes what happened. Jesus has been wrestling in prayer. He walks across the Kidron Valley with his disciples to a garden. But another group journeys to the same place at the same time. We have the Jesus group and the Judas group. Jesus is with his disciples. Judas is with his group of Roman soldiers, police and some Pharisees. It is night-time, so it is dark. But there is a greater darkness than that of the night. Judas unbelievably betrays Jesus with a kiss. A sign of greeting, trust and welcome becomes a sign of desertion and betrayal. The betrayal of an enemy is one thing. The betrayal of a friend is quite another. Peter understandably is not just angry, he's *furious*. He lashes out, not with his fists but with a sword. He strikes the Chief Priest's servant, Malchus, cutting off his right ear.

From what we know of Peter, and based on his track record, I suspect he was aiming at the man's throat, but missed! Peter the volcano had erupted. Once again reaction had preceded reason. This was Peter – instant, spontaneous, sudden, hot-tempered. Do you know anyone like that in your family, among your circle of friends or in your church, cell group or Christian Union? The sort of person who is the first to grab and open the post, who indeed will sometimes run out to the postman because they cannot wait until he comes? They want to be the centre of attention, stand up at the front, feature in all the photographs and be the most prominent person. They are given to exaggeration. A light shower of rain is described as a 'thunderstorm', and a ray of sunshine constitutes a 'heat wave'. They tell the truth, the whole truth and a little bit more than the truth. That was Peter. Yet Jesus looks at him, sees the potential in him and calls him to be a disciple. He doesn't reject him. He trains him, teaches him, prays for him and loves him.

Jesus does the same with us. He is patient with us when others may be impatient. He perseveres with us when others would give up.

Personality
We hear much nowadays about different personality types. Perhaps some of us have experienced the Myers-Briggs

assessment, a process of understanding more fully our own personality type, whether we are introvert or extrovert, and so on. It can be enormously helpful for a couple, a leadership team or any group of people who work together, to walk a Myers-Briggs journey. It will certainly result in a deeper appreciation of how other people 'tick'. Team dynamics and relationships can enter a new depth of quality, leading to more productive and constructive ministry.

In Western society and culture today, there is almost an obsession with self-obsession, self-awareness, self-assessment, self-development, self improvement and so on. We approach such issues in different ways according to our personal beliefs and personalities, but the personality type doesn't matter to Jesus. He loves all of us. The story of Peter illustrates that whoever we are, whatever personality we have, Jesus can take us and change us. This is the message of his dealings with Peter. Jesus Christ can take a person and totally transform that person, yet at the same time use and shape their personality and temperament so that they become more like him. Jesus sees potential and he knows what can happen through one person. He saw in Peter what Peter didn't see in himself. Jesus still looks with those same eyes and sees in us what we cannot see. Thank God for the double vision of Jesus!

Do we have double vision?
As we look at people, do we see them not only as they are, but also as what they may become? Do we see worth and potential? This is the Jesus way, the Christian way. In the very first meeting of Jesus and Peter, we learn this important principle.

We are to have that same double vision and follow Jesus' example. Effective and fruitful Christian workers and leaders see people not just as they are, but as what they can become in Christ . . . people from different racial, political and cultural backgrounds, people with different temperaments and personalities. Is this the kind of double vision which is a mark of our leadership?

Sometimes we reject people in Christian work and ministry. We reach overhasty conclusions about some people and dismiss them too speedily. I wonder how many would have lived differently had they met someone in the church like Jesus, someone who cared for them and saw their potential. How different life would be for some people if, instead of rejection, they had met someone who had looked at them with the eyes of Jesus. Perhaps a more frequent prayer, as we pray for each other, should be that all who claim to follow Jesus will be people who have the double vision of Jesus. Pray too for more double-vision churches!

Pray for more of this kind of vision in each other and in the church worldwide. Each person we meet has potential which is God-given and which can be realized . . .

- the lonely student in lectures who never seems to have a friend;
- the new person in the office who is finding those first few weeks difficult;
- the friend who seems so tactless;
- the work colleague with the big mouth;
- the neighbour who doesn't always say or do the most helpful thing.

We see people differently when we look at them with the eyes of Jesus. He also saw the potential in John. Others might have discarded a disciple who urged Jesus to call fire down from heaven and burn the Samaritans out of one of their villages. It seems hard to believe he is the same person who has become known as an apostle of love. Again and again in his epistles, John encourages us to be generous in our love for one another.

> This is how we know what love is: Jesus Christ laid down his life for us. And we ought to lay down our lives for our brothers and sisters.
> (1 John 3:16)

> Dear children, let us not love with words or speech but with actions and in truth.
> (1 John 3:18)

The old days have gone. Jesus saw what John could become. Barnabas was also a double-vision man. He was willing to run with a fiery intellectual from Tarsus and give him opportunities for ministry when others were more hesitant and cautious. He nurtured the young leader and rejoiced to see him grow and develop. Thank God for Barnabas and for all who practise his ministry of patient encouragement.

With Jesus' kind of potential-spotting vision, opportunities are maximized and unnecessary pain and hurt are minimized. Too many people feel rejection and isolation, and have been wrestling for years with personal pain, because of an absence of patient, compassionate, Christ-like double vision in the lives of those who claim to follow him. Peter met someone who became the greatest influence in his life. He then became someone who influenced and impacted others. God can use us too. He can speak through you and me to influence, impact and inspire others. We will too, when we see as Jesus sees, and when we love as Jesus loves.

Ponder

1. How good are you at seeing the potential in other people?
2. What could you do to become better at being an encourager and a potential-spotter?
3. Who would refer to you as their encourager?
4. Who is God leading you to pray for and invest time in?

Prayer

Thank you, Lord, for seeing potential in me. Thank you that in you I do have a future and a hope. Thank you too for those who affirm and encourage me. Forgive me that sometimes I underestimate the potential in others and in myself. I dismiss people too quickly. Give me the eyes of faith to see potential and thank you for all that can happen in a life surrendered to you. Lord, please give me your double vision. Help me to see with your eyes. Amen.

2. Called to make disciples

As Jesus walked beside the Sea of Galilee, he saw Simon and his brother Andrew casting a net into the lake, for they were fishermen. 'Come, follow me,' Jesus said, 'and I will send you out to fish for people.'

(Mark 1:16–17)

Although Peter was a faux-pas specialist, a slow learner and an embarrassment to himself (and sometimes his friends), Jesus loved him and cared for him deeply. He had a mission for him. Peter was called to be a different kind of fisherman.

On their first encounter, Andrew introduced his brother Peter to Jesus, but on so many occasions in the future, Peter himself would introduce people to Jesus. Luke tells us that on the day of Pentecost when Peter preached, 3,000 were converted and introduced to Jesus. They accepted his message and were baptized. Luke writes that 'many who heard the message believed' (Acts 4:4). In the home of Cornelius the Gentile, Peter spoke of the good news of peace through Jesus Christ and the Holy Spirit came on all who heard the message (Acts 10:34–48).

Peter's priority is also our urgent priority – and the ministry of the church all over the world. Everything we do is to be directed towards introducing people of all ages to Jesus Christ.

Stumbling block or stepping stone?

There are few things more thrilling and exciting than to lead people to Christ. In the twenty-first century, the need is as great as ever. Christ's vision is that we lead more and more inside. It is all too easy to forget what it is like to be on the outside. Worse still, it is appalling when a church has no compassion for those who are on the outside – when the life of the church has become totally inward-looking and when selfish pursuits replace mission adventures. The heart of love has shrivelled. Care isn't there. Hands don't reach out. Compassion has died. 'You are not welcome here!' is the message which others pick up. According to St Paul, a compassionless Christian is a fraud.

> If I speak in the tongues of men or of angels, but do not have love, I am only a resounding gong or a clanging cymbal. If I have the gift of prophecy and can fathom all mysteries and all knowledge, and if I have a faith that can move mountains, but do not have love, I am nothing.
> (1 Corinthians 13:1–2)

A loveless church is a disgrace, for without love we are nothing. In the church, it is the love of Christ which is to control us. His love leads us on. In Peter we see a man who grew in love. He moved from being a stumbling block to being a signpost and a stepping stone, helping others find Christ.

Introduction leads to reproduction

Some think that mission is only about getting people to make a decision to follow Christ. However, the command of Jesus is to nurture and develop disciples. We are to help each other grow in our faith. We are to be fruit-bearing disciples in our character and in our ministry.

I believe God is calling the church today to renew this commitment, which is at the very foundation of the call to discipleship. 'Follow me and I will send you out to fish for people.' It is a call to come to him, to be with him and to proclaim him. It is a call to mission. It is a call to reach out to people of all nations, generations and locations.

How seriously is this taken by his followers? In many churches, for example, there is no longer a children's or youth ministry. Yet many Christians and Christian leaders trace the roots of their journey with Jesus back to their youth or childhood. In other churches, the elderly may as well not exist. Yet in many countries, as people live longer, the percentage of elderly people in the population is increasing. Are we missing strategic and potentially fruitful opportunities of reaching out to these influential age groups? Our call is to all! Everyone is to be reached and in the church, all are called to be involved in the reaching. Jesus has commissioned each member of his church to be a pointer, a signpost to Christ. That's what mission is all about.

Is it your priority to point people towards Jesus Christ, or have you been waylaid or distracted? Have you pursued paths of life, lifestyle and thinking which are not biblical priorities? Peter was beginning to grasp, and later he fully grasped, that to be a Jesus-following disciple is also to be a signpost which points to Jesus. A disciple is someone who gets the point and is a pointer! Christ has caught us and we are to catch others. That fills some of us with excitement, others with fear and apprehension. Perhaps we think, 'I don't want to intrude on the life of someone else. Surely they have their faith and I have mine.' When we think like that, we are missing the calling of

Jesus: 'I will make you . . . ' A core part of his work in us is that he will work through us. He knows our fears and shyness. He promises to be with us. He gives us his Spirit that we might be his witnesses.

Rabbit-hole Christianity

Later in his life, Peter faced the winds and storms of being a fisher of men. Around the fireside, after Jesus was arrested, Peter was away from the other disciples and faced the reality of life outside the group (Luke 22:54–62). He didn't fare very well. He had trouble adjusting to life outside of the cocoon. Peter's witness caved in before a young servant girl. He learnt, albeit painfully, that it is one thing to be a disciple with other disciples, but quite another thing to be a faithful witness among strangers. He failed.

We too have failed in being faithful and courageous witnesses. Yet we are called to be witnesses in our places of work, the roads and streets where we live, in the families and communities of which we are a part. Like Peter, we can struggle when we are outside our areas of comfort. The temptation is to retreat into a comfortable church club. We can hide in a Christian group, but that is not our calling. Ships can stay in a harbour but that is not what ships are for! Rabbit-hole Christianity is not biblical Christianity. A spiritual ghetto may be cosy and warm, but it is not the context of our calling, the arena of our mission nor the area of our service. We are called to face out and go out.

The one who has called us sends us out. The salt cellar may be well insulated and safe, but it is not where we are called to be. We are supposed to out there being salty! We are a new creation but we are still in the box. The church is to be a training ground for mission, not a self-help group absorbed in self-obsessed isolation. Integration and penetration are marks of Christian mission. Unbiblical separation, which in effect is compassionless detachment, is a denial of our DNA. Peter was to step out of his traditional box much further than he could possibly have imagined, when he met with the Roman centurion Cornelius (see Chapter 10 of this book).

In my teenage years, I depended too much on my Christian friends in our school Scripture Union group. When I was not with them I found living as a Christian very difficult. Others have found the same. Fear can kick in, courage dissolves and defeat beckons. Just like Peter, we can cave in. We need to help each other in this area. Those of us in Christian leadership are called to equip those we lead to be refreshingly open about their faith and supernaturally natural in sharing it. We are called to lead by example.

Helping others to grow
'You are only young once but you can remain immature indefinitely!' These were the words on a birthday card sent to me by a friend. They made me laugh, but they also made me think, because they express an uncomfortable truth. They can also apply to the Christian life. A person may have been in the family of God for years but there is little evidence of growth. There is a form of Christianity but a vibrant heart-faith is absent. Steady progress, let alone maturity, is absent.

How do those who profess to be Christians become fruitful and faithful disciples of Jesus? We can be hearers and not doers. We can sing the hymn 'Standing on the promises' when all we are really doing is sitting on the premises! Too easily in the church we can absorb the 'spectator sport' mentality rather than be enthusiastic players in a team. We sit in the seats rather than play on the pitch. How do we enable sons and daughters of God to become servants and disciples?

Investing in others

Some of the most effective leaders in the church worldwide today are those who, alongside a wider ministry, are committed to a more focused ministry in the strategic development of a few . . . just like Jesus was with Peter and the core disciples. What a model for developing any kind of Christian work, whether it is a church, Bible study group, student group or Scripture Union Group. We all minister in circles of influence. The reality is that we minister to various sizes of groups of people but, like Jesus, are you training inner cores who receive particular training and more personal input? This is real discipling and leadership training. It is essential if any Christian work is to grow. This is the Jesus way.

Grow as you go, go as you grow

In many parts of the church today, becoming a 'reflective practitioner' is frequently espoused as a desirable and effective model of Christian leadership and theological training. It is a model we see practised in the ministry of Jesus. He calls his disciples to him and he sends them out. They return from their mission and ministry, and what happens next? They are not left high and dry . . . emotionally high and internally dry. Jesus avoids such an outcome. He ensures that together, they reflect on their recent events and experiences.

For example, in Mark 6, we read of Jesus sending out the twelve disciples two by two. He gave them clear instructions. After their mission adventure, 'The apostles gathered around Jesus and reported to him all they had done and taught' (Mark 6:30).

Another example occurs immediately after the transfiguration. A man approaches Jesus. He cries out for mercy because his son is possessed with an evil spirit. He says, 'I asked your disciples to drive out the spirit, but they could not'

(Mark 9:18). Jesus rebukes the spirit and the boy is dramatically healed. The reflection and interaction between the disciples and Jesus takes place in private. 'After Jesus had gone indoors, his disciples asked him privately, "Why couldn't we drive it out?" He replied, "This kind can come out only by prayer"' (Mark 9:28–29). Interestingly, following this encounter they were on the road again and Mark comments on Jesus, 'Leaving there, they went through Galilee. He didn't want anyone to know their whereabouts, for he wanted to teach his disciples' (Mark 9:30–31, *The Message*).

All the time, Jesus was training his disciples. He was committed to their lifelong learning. They knew he was a teacher who never missed an opportunity to teach. They learnt as they listened to him. They thought as well as acted. They acted as well as thought. Being a disciple is both a personal and corporate activity. Many mission activities and outreach events in and through the church have never been in the context of lifelong learning and practical reflection. But this kind of discipleship dynamic can contribute enormously to personal growth in the life of a Christian and congregational growth in the life of a church, Christian mission or organization. Jesus calls us to make disciples and be fishers of men.

A call to catch

Have you neglected Christ's call to catch, his passion to teach, his mission to save? Jesus hasn't! People are not turkeys, even though we do squabble at times. People are made in God's image. Christ died for each person. That's how valuable we are to him. All are equal. Is that truth embedded in your heart and soul? Do you despise the small things, small numbers and ordinary people? We want the high-powered and the big names. We give preference to certain people. That's not how Jesus thinks. His call to Peter and to all of us couldn't be simpler and clearer. Peter heard the call, followed the caller and moved to being a signpost.

He did take up Christ's challenge and he became a 'fisher of men'. He became fearless in his witness, faithful in adversity and loyal to his Lord. Whatever else we admire in Peter, we cannot fail to admire his openness to learn. What a model! With clarity, compassion and conviction, he pointed people to Jesus. Our calling is the same . . . nothing less and nothing more. As others look at our lives, they are to see something of Jesus because our lives are signposts pointing towards him. No matter how we feel about ourselves and others, the truth is that Jesus Christ can use us. We matter to him! Hallelujah!

Ponder

1. Who do you know who might be ready to be pointed towards Jesus this week? Which approach is going to be the most helpful to them and the most sensitive and effective?
2. Who do you know who has made a decision for Christ, but is not yet growing as a disciple? How can you help them continue their journey?
3. Ask God to increase your love towards those who don't yet know him.
4. How can you better prepare those you lead for the rigours and rough edges of life outside the faith community?

The following are some words preached by Charles Haddon Spurgeon on this call of Christ

Go to work, you who would be fishers of men, and yet feel your insufficiency. You that have no strength, attempt this divine work. Your Master's strength will be seen when your own has all gone. A fisherman is a dependent person, he must look up for success every time he puts the net down; but still he is a trustful person, and therefore he casts in the net joyfully.

Prayer

Lord Jesus, forgive me that sometimes I overlook people who might be ready to be pointed towards you. Help me to see what you see. I want to be a signpost, not an obstacle. I want to be a stepping stone, not a stumbling block. Enable me to point and to lead others to you. Amen.

3. Feed my sheep

When they had finished eating, Jesus said to Simon Peter, 'Simon son of John, do you love me more than these?'

'Yes, Lord,' he said, 'you know that I love you.'

Jesus said, 'Feed my lambs.'

Again Jesus said, 'Simon son of John, do you truly love me?'

He answered, 'Yes, Lord, you know that I love you.'

Jesus said, 'Take care of my sheep.'

The third time he said to him, 'Simon son of John, do you love me?'

Peter was hurt because Jesus asked him the third time, 'Do you love me?' He said, 'Lord, you know all things; you know that I love you.'

Jesus said, 'Feed my sheep' . . . Then he said to him, 'Follow me!'

(John 21:15–17, 19)

Someone summarized Peter's life in this way. Peter at the fire! Peter in the fire! Peter on fire! Although succinct, these sentences do highlight something of the significant change which Peter experienced in his life. They also touch on the fact that Peter the fiery character became Peter the on-fire disciple. He had been in the fire at the fire when he denied Jesus (see Chapter 7 of this book). Now, some time later, he is at a fire once again. This time he has an encounter which is pivotal in his development. It is to be a life-changing conversation with the risen Jesus.

From time to time in the Western world, usually at a time of some emergency or crisis, we will see harrowing pictures from other parts of the world. They focus on emaciated bodies, skeletal figures, the victims of chronic food shortages and frightening famine. Millions of pounds, euros and dollars are given as charitable donations. A channel of aid opens up because of generous giving from different individuals, countries and many churches . . . and rightly so! There is something wrong if, as Christians, we are not moved with compassion into loving action when we see the protruding ribs of starving people and the heart-rending sight of dying children. Starvation in the twenty-first century is an obscenity. We in the church are called to action. Such suffering causes pain in God's heart. The church is called to be a voice for the voiceless and a defender of the weak. We are called to love our neighbour.

Another kind of starvation
But there is another kind of starvation, which is causing pain in the heart of God. He sees the skeletons of the underfed. He hears the cries of those without food. He feels their hunger pains. He is moved with compassion when he sees people as harassed and helpless, like sheep without a shepherd. Whatever the dimensions of physical need, spiritual need is of gargantuan proportions. There is a spiritual need which breaks the heart of God. The compassion in the heart of God, the vision of people needing to be fed, the restoration of a repentant

rebel . . . all form the context of this early-morning breakfast conversation 2,000 years ago. The shores of the Sea of Galilee are the open-air classroom where Peter learns another vitally important lesson. His mission is unmistakeably identified, as Jesus highlights and clarifies Peter's specific calling. Peter is to feed and care for God's people.

It is God's will that his people are fed. They are to become strong, mature and compassionate, a people who know their God, who can give a reason for the hope that is within them. They are to be a people of understanding. God wants sheep that are fed, not a church of anaemic, spiritually anorexic and starving disciples.

Most shepherds shear their sheep once a year and feed them daily. In some churches it is the other way round. The sheep are shorn every Sunday and rarely fed! Jesus did not say to Peter, 'Fleece my sheep.' He said, 'Feed my lambs. Take care of my sheep.'

A starved soul results in an impoverished witness. Teaching is an artery in the heart of the church. One of the marks of the early church was they devoted themselves to the apostles' teaching. Wherever the apostles went, they taught the word of God. For a whole year, Saul and Barnabas taught the new Christians in Antioch and helped establish them in the faith. Peter really heard what Jesus said and his ministry was one of teaching. We see it in his sermons in Acts and in his two epistles. His sermons draw heavily from the Old Testament Scriptures. On the day of Pentecost he links what is happening to words of the prophet Joel. He speaks of David and quotes the Psalms. His vivid presentation is firmly rooted in God's revelation.

A wholesome diet

Jesus calls, in every generation, people like Peter who will feed others. Jesus calls teachers who will enable others to become strong, healthy and effective in their respective lives and ministries. In the church of Christ, some are called to be proclaimers and channels of life-changing truths in the church. And what is the food with which the sheep are to be fed? It is a wholesome diet. It is not a preacher's particular fad or hobbyhorse. It is not our opinions and ideas. It is the whole counsel of God, the word of truth and life. We teach what God has revealed, not what we have cleverly invented. In his second letter Peter wrote:

> We did not follow cleverly devised stories when we told you about the coming of our Lord Jesus Christ in power, but we were eyewitnesses of his majesty . . .
>
> Above all, you must understand that no prophecy of Scripture came about by the prophet's own interpretation of things. For prophecy never had its origin in the human will, but prophets, though human, spoke from God as they were carried along by the Holy Spirit . . .
>
> I want you to recall the words spoken in the past by the holy prophets and the command given by our Lord and Saviour through your apostles.
>
> (2 Peter 1:16, 20, 21 and 3:2)

One of the greatest and most pressing needs in the worldwide church today is that the word of God is taught, explained, expounded and applied in a life-related and life-impacting way. We live in a world that is increasingly ignorant of biblical truth, devoid of biblical knowledge and unaware of God's unique revelation. In my lifetime I have witnessed in Ireland and in the United Kingdom such a significant decrease in the knowledge and understanding of the Scriptures. In many of the popular TV quiz shows, it is often the biblical questions that remain unanswered. There is also misunderstanding of what the Bible teaches. How often people have said to me with impressive authority, 'The Bible says charity begins at home.' It doesn't! I have searched the Scriptures and it isn't there! It is not going over the top to say that the words of Amos apply accurately today. There is 'a famine of hearing the words of the Lord' (Amos 8:11). If ever the ministry of faithful teaching and preaching was needed, it is needed now. I am utterly convinced that a Bible-based ministry which is releasing the word of God into the people of God will have a dynamic impact in the world of God.

I came across the following anonymous article:

A young pastor was being interviewed for a job. An older deacon asked him: 'How well do you know your Bible, lad?' 'Oh, really well,' the young man replied. And to show this he told the story of the prodigal son:

'There was a man of the Pharisees named Nicodemus who went to Jericho by night. And he fell upon stony ground and the thorns choked him half to death. The next morning Solomon and his wife Gomorrah came by and took him down to the ark so that Moses could care for him. But as he was going through the eastern gate toward the ark, his hair was caught in a limb, and he hung there forty days and forty nights. Afterward he was hungry and the ravens came and fed him. The next day three wise men came and carried him down to the boat dock where he caught a ship to Nineveh. When he got there he saw Delilah sitting on a wall.

'And Nicodemus said, "Throw her down off the wall." And the wise man said, "How many times shall we throw her down? Seven times seven?" And Nicodemus replied, "Nay, but seventy times seven." And they threw her down 490 times. She burst asunder in their midst, and they picked up twelve baskets of fragments. My question is, whose wife will she be in the resurrection?'

The elderly deacon said to the others, 'Friends, I think we ought to call him. He's awfully young, but he really knows his Bible.'

It is a funny story, but it illustrates a tragic reality.

An endangered species

The church of God has the word of God in its veins. We don't need a transfusion of any other core truths. They are here in Scripture. What we do need is to continue applying ourselves to working out ways of presenting God's truth to the literate and illiterate, the academic and the non-academic, in ways that are arresting, gripping and penetrating. In God's purposes, teaching is to stretch and renew the mind and to feed the soul. One young person, who had gone to live in a major city, visited several churches, of different traditions, and her experiences led her to say, 'I now go to the theatre to think and I go to church to be entertained.' May God forgive us!

In seeking to relate to children and young people, we must remember that God's unique revelation is remarkably relevant to all ages and abilities. Sometimes there is a danger that relevance can supersede revelation. It must never be forgotten that it is *God's truth* which sets people free. His word is about meat as well as milk. Preaching and teaching are to be contemporary but not simplistic. The twenty-first century is now the context for letting the Bible loose. As the famous Baptist preacher Charles Haddon Spurgeon said, 'The Bible is like a lion, you don't have to defend it, you just let it loose.' Like some species of wild cats, a Bible that bites into lives and cultures is an endangered species. Our priority is to seek ways of opening up the Bible in a way that will feed people and not cause them to choke. God's word is intended to free people to serve in a contemporary culture, not freeze them in a time warp.

Why have we made teaching the Bible so dull and blunted its relevance? How sad that preachers and teachers can take the most wonderful, astonishing and exciting book, and reduce learning from it to a dreary, painful endurance test. Dryden the poet parodies the making of a preacher in these terms:

> The midwife laid her hand on his thick skull
> With this prophetic blessing – 'Be thou dull.'
> (Dryden, *The Second Part of Absalom and Achitophel*)

May God forgive us if we sponsor boredom! May God forgive us when the teachers no longer teach and the preachers no longer preach, when the pulpit becomes a place for religious waffle and a charitable humanism, and when a mild-mannered preacher speaks to mild-mannered people in a mild-mannered way. A spiritually starving world needs to hear words of *life*. We do not live by bread alone but by every word which proceeds from the mouth of God. Anxious dying people need the kiss of life from the prince of peace and the king of life. The Holy Spirit, the life-giver, always draws attention to the one who is 'the way and the truth and the life' (John 14:6). The moods and fashions of culture and society will change, but God's truth does not change. The command of Jesus to Peter is as relevant today as it was when first spoken by the lakeside. It is a command to the church: 'Feed my sheep!'

Ponder

1. Thank the Lord for the people who have taught you. Pray for those called to preach and teach.

2. From where are you receiving teaching at this time? How can you maximize opportunities to be fed on the word of God? Consider how you might make use of personal Bible study, reading, DVDs and CDs, small groups, sermons, Christian festivals.
3. Could God be calling you to be a teacher?

Prayer

Lord, grant that in the church today we may discover a renewed commitment to liberate your living word. Forgive us when we peddle our own inadequate ideas. We pray that as your word is taught, the lives of individual Christians will be impacted profoundly, local churches will be strengthened substantially and local communities will be radically transformed. Lord, let your word loose in our midst! May the days of famine be over and may your word be taught and lived. Amen.

Keeping focus
*So many voices
clamour for attention.
How can we hear the
whispers of God?*

4. Help! I'm too busy!

[Jesus] took Peter, John and James with him and went up onto a mountain to pray.

(Luke 9:28)

Frequently I listen to Christian people who are excited . . . but exhausted. Their lives are busy with endless activity. They are excited about God's purposes but they are deeply tired, physically and emotionally. They are serving as church workers, missionaries, committee members, church members, youth workers or Christian leaders. One leader said, 'I pray but I don't think my prayers go higher than the ceiling.' Another said, 'Quite frankly, I'm exhausted. My wife never sees me. My children have an absent father. I cannot go on like this.' Something vital is missing. They are feeding others but feel malnourished themselves. Life seems to be out of control.

I know the experience only too well myself. I have been there . . . giving but not receiving, giving out in ministry and service, but not taking in that which will sustain me for the long haul. I am called to be a Christian teacher, but I forget that I too need to be taught. I am regularly preparing spiritual food for others, but I am not being fed myself. Is it surprising then when I sense I am not growing? Why should I be shocked when I feel the way I do? The bottom line is that I am mal-nourished! In my excessive busyness I have cut myself off from God's extravagant and endless supply lines. His resources are untapped and I am trapped in a cul-de-sac of my own making. He *is* with me, but to all intent and purposes I am not with him. I have rushed ahead. I have stepped out of line. I am running on empty and I haven't seen it. I am telling others about Jesus the friend, but he has become a stranger in my own life and experience. The pressing reality is that I need to do something about it. I can blame others, but I am the only one who can take steps to address the busyness, manage the diary and learn to say no.

If these symptoms seem familiar to you, then it can be very helpful to chat with someone you know and trust who will walk with you in this process. It may be that you also need to look at your personal devotional life. You may have been all action but to the neglect of intimacy. Your paradigm has been working *for* him. You have to learn the priority of being *with* him – just as Peter did.

Being with Jesus

The story in Luke 9 is one of both transfiguration and trans-formation. Jesus invited three disciples to be *with him*. He invites us to do the same . . . to draw aside and enjoy his presence with us.

> Jesus . . . took Peter, John and James with him and went up onto a mountain to pray. As he was praying, the appearance of his face changed, and his clothes became as bright as a flash of lightning. Two men, Moses and Elijah, appeared in glorious splendour, talking with Jesus. They spoke about his

departure, which he was about to bring to fulfilment at
Jerusalem. Peter and his companions were very sleepy, but
when they became fully awake, they saw his glory and the
two men standing with him.
(Luke 9:28–32)

Jesus was in the full flow of his three years of public ministry.
He had been teaching and preaching, healing and helping,
ministering to individuals and crowds. He had been engaged
in the exacting but strategic task of training his disciples. This
unique transfiguration event is a superb illustration of a
learning model which is effective and life-changing.

Balance and blending

At certain points in the Gospel stories, Jesus gives particular
attention to these three men: Peter, John and James. Why did
Jesus take them aside from the busyness and pressures of
public ministry? Clearly it is because he the Teacher is teaching.
In the life and ministry of Jesus there was a balance and
blending of public ministry and personal renewal, of work
and rest, of corporate activity and private personal prayer.
Luke captures this tellingly in his Gospel: 'Crowds of people
came to hear him and be healed of their sicknesses. But Jesus
often withdrew to lonely places and prayed' (Luke 5:15–16).
We neglect this balance and blending at our peril. Too many
in their Christian lives and leadership have neglected this Jesus
way and the consequences have been tragic.

The reality is that often, without intending it, our lives are
driven by deadlines rather than refreshed by lifelines. The
blending I see present in the life of Jesus can be absent in my
life. Instead of wholesome rhythm, there is wearisome rut.
The rhythm of work and rest in his ministry is a rut of just
work in my own.

Come

It is indisputable that one of the greatest dangers in Christian
service is to neglect our communion with Christ – to clothe
and feed our bodies but neglect our own souls. Over and over
again the neglect is not because of a crisis of faith but simply
because we are too busy. The well-known Puritan leader
Richard Baxter once said, 'Take heed to yourselves lest you
perish while you call upon others to take heed of perishing,
lest you famish yourselves while you prepare their food.'

I love the story, told by Mrs Lettie Cowman, which is quoted
by Gordon MacDonald in his book *Restoring Your Spiritual
Passion*. The story comes from African colonial history:

> 'In the deep jungles of Africa, a traveller was making a long
> trek. Coolies had been engaged from a tribe to carry the loads.
> The first day they marched rapidly and went far. The traveller
> had high hopes of a speedy journey. But the second morning
> they refused to move. For some strange reason they just sat
> and rested. On enquiry as to this strange behaviour, the
> traveller was informed that they had gone too fast the first day,
> and that they were waiting for their souls to catch up with
> their bodies.' Then Mrs Cowman concludes with this
> penetrating exhortation, 'This whirling rushing life which so
> many of us live does for us what that first march did for those
> poor jungle tribesmen. The difference: they knew what they
> needed to restore life's balance; too often we do not.'

We all need times of allowing our souls to catch up with our
bodies, times of personal refreshment and renewal, times of
recharging the spiritual batteries. Jesus taught these disciples
the priorities of balance, blending, reflection, prayer, *time* with
himself. I wonder if this is the most important issue we need
to deal with at this time in our lives. Neglecting to do so is not

an option. Years later, as he reflected, Peter wrote, 'Come to
him . . .' (1 Peter 2:4). Jesus says, 'Come to me . . . and I will
give you rest' (Matthew 11:28).

Times apart

For most people, there are special places in life . . .

- that spot where we first saw the person to whom we are
  now married;
- a specific location where we heard either very good
  news or very bad news;
- the place where we first met Jesus.

Perhaps for those who are keen on sport, one of these places
may be a national sports stadium where our national team
or favourite team recorded a sensational victory. It is so special
it has almost become a shrine! It may be Lansdowne Road
for rugby fans, or Wembley Stadium or Wimbledon. For
keen golfers it may be Augusta or St Andrews. All of these
places are packed with highly emotional and unforgettable
memories.

In different seasons of our life, we all have special places. It
is the same in the history and life of the people of God. There
have always been special places in the story of his people.

The Lord is in this place

For Noah, the mountains of Ararat were a special place. For
Abraham, the region of Moriah and the great trees of Mamre
were special places. For Jacob, a special place was Bethel,
where he had that amazing dream.

> When Jacob awoke from his sleep, he thought, 'Surely the
> Lord is in this place, and I was not aware of it.' He was afraid

and said, 'How awesome is this place! This is none other than
the house of God; this is the gate of heaven.'
(Genesis 28:16–17)

How could Jacob ever forget what happened in that place? An
encounter with God of the most amazing, breathtaking kind.
Bethlehem, Nazareth, the Sea of Galilee, the Garden of
Gethsemane, Calvary . . . these are all special places in the life
of Jesus and in the history of the church. They are such an
important part of the Christian story and the church's memory.
In Peter's family, how would his mother-in-law ever forget the
place where Jesus came to her and healed her? Others gazed.
He was unfazed. All were amazed. This was a place they
would always associate with healing and miracle.

Some Christian traditions are strong on special symbols and
regular pilgrimages to special places. Others don't emphasize
such practices but do practise them. Tours are organized to
the Holy Land. Visits are made to where a famous preacher
was born, worked or died. Prayer mountains in South Korea
have become a significant part of the prayer life of growing
churches and individuals. In all of our lives, God has worked
in remarkable ways and spoken into our lives clearly and
unmistakeably. The transfiguration was not just an example
of taking special time to be with Jesus. It was also an
opportunity for space – away from the humdrum realities and
pressures of everyday life. Peter and his friends would never
forget this mountain experience. That's for certain.

The mountain is traditionally thought to be Mount Tabor,
but it may have been one of the ridges of Hermon. In terms
of what we can learn from this incident, the precise location
doesn't really matter. What does matter is that these three
disciples had a deep encounter with the Lord and for them
this would always be a special place.

Bethel . . . Galilee . . . Castlerock

The name Castlerock may well not mean anything to you, but for me it is a special place. For many holidaymakers, Castlerock is a beautiful and scenic seaside resort on the north coast of Northern Ireland. For me it is the place where as a young boy of twelve I gave my life unreservedly and whole-heartedly to Jesus Christ. It was 1961 and I was attending a Scripture Union Camp for young teenage boys. Late one night, as I lay in a top bunk bed, I knew that the Lord was knocking on the door of my life. He was standing waiting, on the outside. He knocked with love and called me to follow him. I opened the door of my life and with utter sincerity and from the depth of my young heart, I confessed my sin and asked Jesus Christ to come in. He did! I knew he had dealt with my sin on the cross. I knew he was alive. With deep thankfulness and a genuine willingness I surrendered my life to him and his will. For me it was a life-defining turning point. I never pass through Castlerock without thinking back to that time. For me it is a special place. I can never thank God enough for what happened there. It was not on a mountain or on a beach like Peter. It was not on a Roman road like Saul of Tarsus but it was my Damascus road. I saw Jesus as I had never seen him before. I would never be the same again.

Damascus Road . . . Emmaus Road

For some others, their Christian journey is more like an Emmaus road than a Damascus road. It is more of an evolution than a revolution – a long road rather than a crossroads. However, the outcome is the same. Jesus draws near to us and we are changed. It cannot be pinpointed to a specific time or place. That is OK. The main thing is that Jesus is walking with us. As he does, we will have special places along the journey

and there will be special people who also walk with us for part
of the journey or for most of it.

As we reflect on these events and experiences in our own
lives, very often we recognize that other people were involved.
They served as friends, facilitators, helpers. Without their wise
and sensitive input, we might very well have struggled and
missed an opportunity. Their faithfulness has ensured the
creation of a special place in our lives. Jesus did that for these
three disciples.

It is my impression that men, on the whole, find it more
difficult than women to open their hearts to someone else.
Men talk about sport and work, but going deeper than that
can be quite a challenge. Is it something to do with independence, being macho, seeing sharing as a sign of weakness,
fearing to appear weak? Whatever the reason, we miss out on
so much if we ignore the kind of friendships Jesus experienced
and modelled for others. We see this quality of friendship at
different points in the Bible. I have always been impressed by
the supportive friendship between David and Jonathan – for
example, when David was in hiding from Jonathan's erratic
and sometimes violent father, Saul:

> And Saul's son Jonathan went to David at Horesh and helped
> him find strength in God. 'Don't be afraid,' he said. 'My father
> Saul will not lay a hand on you. You will be king over Israel,
> and I will be second to you. Even my father Saul knows this.'
> (1 Samuel 23:16–17)

Jonathan didn't come to defend David. He came, as his friend,
to help him find his strength in God. He encouraged him
not to be afraid. I have found, at different times in my life,
that God has sent someone, often surprisingly, who has
spoken a word which has been exactly right for that particular

time and situation. I call those people 'God's angels', for they take us unawares.

A place provider

Any of us can be such angels to others. We can create special time and places for other people. We can enable people to step away from their everyday settings – whether for a walk and talk together, a group event or an organized retreat. In future years, as others look back, will they point to a conversation with us as a turning point? Will they thank God for the time we listened and helped them on their journey? The writer of Proverbs says, 'The purposes of a man's heart are deep waters, but one who has insight draws them out' (Proverbs 20:5). We can be those people of understanding. We can offer big ears and have a big heart, helping others to find forgiveness and freedom. It is a high calling and an immense privilege. We can help create special places for others which will have an eternal significance. For them, those places will not be about transfiguration, but about transformation. Both are about Jesus.

What about . . .

- getting together regularly with a group of people to whom you can give, and from whom you can receive?
- meeting up with someone just to listen to them, express appreciation, and give encouragement?
- sending an email or writing a letter to someone else who is in leadership? Some missionaries and leaders are lonely and long for some contact with someone who cares.
- taking a small group away as Jesus did? You may choose to take them to a conference, a course, a retreat or simply to have some time together in a focused way.

- meeting someone for a coffee or a meal and having a long and unhurried time of strengthening one another in God? You can share stories and struggles.

For Peter, James and John, the memories would have flooded back each time they passed this mountain. It was a place of replenishment and encounter. It was a special place, for there they saw Jesus as they had never seen him before. This was another defining and refining time in the life of Peter.

Ponder

1. Think of a special place or time in your life. Thank the Lord for what he did there. Pray for any others who were a part of it. Pray too that we will be used by the Lord to facilitate the creation of special places in the lives of others.
2. How can you retain or restore balance in your life?
3. Is there someone who can help you sort out your priorities and keep you accountable?
4. Do you need to build in some time away and spend time with some special people, or alone?
5. Is there anyone that God is drawing you to particularly support and mentor in their work–rest balance and discipleship?

Prayer

Lord, you know the excitement I feel and the weariness I have sometimes felt. Lord, thank you for leading us into times of refreshment. Thank you for your green pastures and still waters. You know the strategic importance of time apart. You also know the deep needs in my heart and life. I have so much to learn from you. I desire to be not just better equipped for the Lord's work, but closer to you, the Lord of the work. Draw me closer to you. These three disciples were three of your special people. Thank you that I am also one of your special people. Never let me forget it! Amen.

5. Listen to him . . . focus on him

As the men were leaving Jesus, Peter said to him, 'Master, it is good for us to be here. Let us put up three shelters – one for you, one for Moses and one for Elijah.' (He did not know what he was saying.)

While he was speaking, a cloud appeared and covered them, and they were afraid as they entered the cloud. A voice came from the cloud, saying, 'This is my Son, whom I have chosen; listen to him.'

(Luke 9:33–35)

All ears

When one of our daughters was very young, she saw her granny do something that she had never seen before. She watched in childish wonder and bewilderment at this new thing. It was truly sensational through the eyes of a little child. Granny took her teeth out and put them in again. Having observed, several times, this unique act of magic, our inquisitive daughter enquired, 'Granny, may I ask you a question?' Her granny replied, 'Of course you can.' The penetrating question followed: 'Can you take your ears off as well?'

It was an intelligent question. After all, if teeth can come out, surely ears can come off too! I often think that there are times in our Christian lives when we take our ears off and we do not listen to God. We can be present in a service of worship, but we have left our ears at home. We read the Bible but our minds are all over the place and in reality our ears are closed. Yet at the transfiguration, there is this powerful message from God the Father as he refers to God the Son: 'Listen to him!' In the church of Jesus Christ we are called to be listeners.

Listen to him

Of all the things God could have said from heaven, his message was: 'Listen!' This has always been a message from the Lord to those he loves. Repeatedly in the history of his people, God asks them to listen. Sadly, and with astounding and frightening consistency, his people did not listen to his voice, but to other voices. They went their own way. They sowed the seeds of arrogant independence. Sometimes even the priests and prophets did not listen, and the leaders were deaf. The consequences were always disastrous.

According to the Scriptures, one of the marks of a true prophet is that he listens to God. By contrast, the false prophets made up their own messages, declared their own opinions and did not listen to the Lord. They listened to other voices. God had to say of them, with a heavy heart:

> Do not listen to what the prophets are prophesying to you;
>   they fill you with false hopes.
> They speak visions from their own minds,
>   not from the mouth of the LORD . . .
> But which of them has stood in the council of the LORD
>   to see or to hear his word?
> (Jeremiah 23:16, 18)

Their basic problem was quite simple – they did not pay attention. This was at the root of their deceit. The true prophet hears God's word and passes it on. In order to really hear, we too must listen. The true prophet is a listener – an attentive, responsive, obedient listener.

Clamouring voices

Whatever our country, culture or background, we are exposed to so many voices. We have voices seeking to seduce us into giving ourselves to addiction, affluence, selfish pleasure, illegal profit, harmful habits, destructive behaviour and sloppy service. Which voice has priority? To whom are you listening? It's important because the voices you listen to determine the choices you make.

An ear witness

Hearing the voice of God on the mountain clearly left its mark on Peter. He was both an ear witness and an eye witness. In one of his epistles, he emphasizes that our faith is not about clever stories of our own invention; rather it is about God's voice and revelation. Peter's teaching was built on the sturdy foundation of having listened to God's voice:

> We did not follow cleverly devised stories when we told you about the coming of our Lord Jesus Christ in power, but we were eye-witnesses of his majesty. He received honour and glory from God the Father when the voice came to him from the Majestic Glory, saying, 'This is my Son, whom I love; with him I am well pleased.' We ourselves heard this voice that came from heaven when we were with him on the sacred mountain.
>
> (2 Peter 1:16–18)

In a society where openness to various voices is common, we do well to hear and heed these words of Peter.

Keep your ears on!

We need to make a priority of listening to God in our own personal lives and in our committees and councils. Do we set aside time to pray and to listen to the Lord at our meetings? Sometimes we can lose our way, spiritually and strategically, because we have ceased to listen to the Lord. We forge ahead. We rush forwards (or backwards). We make our plans. We devise our programmes, but like the false prophets, we have not listened to the Lord. We arrange the agenda and then ask the Lord to bless it. Committee meetings often open with a short and hurried prayer. Why not ask two or three people to open with a prayer? (Warn them beforehand.) Why not pause during the meeting for prayer regarding a particular item? Always at the beginning of our quarterly Diocesan Council meetings, I will lead in a short devotional of Bible reading, brief exposition and prayer. One of the top priorities in the church is to encourage and nurture good listening in the church. Keep your ears on! Hear what the Spirit is saying to the Church, and to each one of us today!

I wonder if you listened more to God's voice, would you speak less but achieve more as one of his kingdom's voices? Now, there's a thought!

Listening to God, listening to people

Listening to God means that we will also listen to other people. We are part of a tradition which listens to the voices of individuals. People of all ages can become the victims of loveless voices and foolish choices. Elderly people can feel they don't matter any more. Other people are too busy to spend time with them. Families have forgotten them. For some, the sound of another human voice, other than what they hear on the radio or TV, is a rare experience. An inner voice tells them that nobody cares. Is it surprising, then, that there are now more counsellors than soldiers in the UK, and that those in the caring professions discover again and again that the real issue is that people want and need someone to listen to them?

Howling at the moon

Do we take time, for example, to listen to the voices of children and young people, and to understand their world? I read the following in *Time* magazine:

'This is a disgusting generation. It's a disgusting time to live in. It's boring,' says Alexandra Lynn, who is 15 going on 25, as she languidly smokes a cigarette with a gaggle of similarly jaded teens in Greenwich Village's Washington Square Park on a sultry Wednesday night.

'The 90s is an exhausted decade. There's nothing to look for and nowhere to go. This generation really hasn't got any solid ground. I mean, the 60s had solid ground, but that's gone now. The only thing we have to rebel against is rebelling itself,' says Alexandra. 'Everything has been done and everything has been stood for, everything has been fought over and basically it's now like there's no more debate . . . what is there to do? There's nothing to do, there's nothing even to look at, because the shock value is gone.'

Her buddy Harry Siegel elaborates on this point. 'The ability to howl at the moon has been lost,' he laments, 'the counter-culture has been absorbed by the culture. The blue hair and the pierced nipples are trite and no one pays them any notice. Nothing is outside the fold.'[1]

No solid ground! There's nothing to build on which will last. There's nothing to stand on which is steady. That's how so many people think and feel. It is not an occasional thought. It is a daily reality. It's a struggle to keep going. Life just seems to be about push-push-push and duty-duty-duty.

Jesus gave Peter solid ground. He gave him a rock to build his life on. He would use him to be a rock to others. Peter had never met anyone like this before. For the first time, he sensed that someone really believed in him and cared for him. He didn't sense rejection when Jesus was around. He knew he was valued . . . and so are we! That is one of the great truths of the gospel. When released into the mind and heart of a human being, it is like an explosion of life.

The words of men and women will not transform anyone or anything eternally. The word of God will, for God's words are words of life. Peter knew this, as he demonstrated at one time in the ministry of Jesus.

> From this time many of his disciples turned back and no longer followed him.
> 'You do not want to leave too, do you?' Jesus asked the Twelve.
> Simon Peter answered him, 'Lord, to whom shall we go? You have the words of eternal life.'
> (John 6:66–68)

Good for Peter! He had grasped a fundamental truth and he expressed it. Listening to God is a pathway to life.

Be clear

More than anything else, people need to hear God's voice. *God's* word is totally life-related. It scratches where we itch. We don't change in order to be relevant. We speak God's word and seek to live it because it is relevant. Did not Jesus say, 'Man shall not live by bread alone, but by every word that proceeds from the mouth of God'? But people need to hear God's inspired word in a way that they will understand, not in a language which is foreign to them. One of the principles which guided Cranmer in his crafting of the Anglican liturgy was that it would be in a language which was understood by people. In some groups we speak only 'the language of Zion' but those listening don't come from Zion.

I have attended many conferences where translators have been employed. It is crucial that they are there. Why? So that all present can not only hear but also understand. It is frustrating when the presentation is in a language we do not understand. It is a transforming experience to hear the presentation in your own language. How much more important is it that the gospel is communicated in ways that are intelligible, rational, relevant, lucid and uncluttered? People made in God's image need to hear God's voice in a language that is clear and contemporary. The use of visuals, the arts, drama, DVDs and film clips are just some ways which will resonate without sacrificing the substance of God's good news. Without realizing it, we can send mixed signals because of our familiarity with particular theological words and concepts. We can confuse people so that they are not quite sure what we are saying. Perhaps they are just beginning to understand when we make an attempt to clarify what we are saying and then they are more confused! I saw a sign outside a church which read, 'Come to our Healing Service! You won't get better!' What exactly does this mean? How much clearer and more probing was another sign I saw which read, 'If God is your co-pilot, swap seats!'

Learning the language

Our task is to channel God's word into people's lives. We are
called to be at the forefront of communicating God's word in
a highly imaginative, innovative, biblical and contemporary
way. Is that still a top priority in our church or student group?
It is all too easy to be stuck in a particular form or format. It
can be more comfortable to stick to the familiar. However, in
forms and expressions of communication, our culture moves
on and we can stand still. We speak a language people do not
understand, the language of the past. We appear detached and
irrelevant. We seem to be people of a different age. We cease
to be like the Word made flesh who dwelt among us. The
language and terminology of our message is so fossilized that
the people the Lord loves are ostracized. 'If the horse is dead,
dismount!' is how one person graphically expressed it. Some
Christian groups are so chained to misguided understandings
of faithfulness to the gospel that our voice is no longer heard
in the community. Quite simply, people cannot understand
us. We are trapped in an ecclesiastical Dr Who time machine.
If we think of being dropped in a foreign country not knowing
a word of the language, nor knowing the culture and customs,
that is how many people today feel about the church.

God has spoken. His voice has been heard. The records are
there. The message is clear. No matter how plausible, additions
and subtractions are not options. They are 'invented stories'.
The voice of his majesty still has unique authority; it is final.
Are you listening, and are you helping others to listen too?

Focus on him

In Mark's account of the transfiguration story, he writes that
'they no longer saw anyone with them except Jesus' (Mark
9:8). Another version of the Bible, the New King James
Version, translates Matthew's version of this verse: 'They saw

no-one but Jesus only' (Matthew 17:8). These disciples were learning on this mountain not just to listen to a special voice, but also to look at a special person. Sometimes in the rough and tumble of ministry and leadership, we lose our focus. We take our eyes off Jesus and our commitment becomes shallow, our self-discipline dissipates and our love grows cold. Yet our deepest and greatest needs are met in Jesus Christ. Each day in our Christian lives, we need to look again and see Jesus only. Sometimes when I go into a pulpit to preach, I will come across these words written on the pulpit: 'Sir, we would see Jesus.' How appropriate they are, how right and how necessary they are, for in him and him alone we have life! With him are unsearchable riches and in him are inexhaustible resources.

One wish

Once the famous evangelist, D. L. Moody, asked Fanny Crosby, the well-known hymn writer, what her wish would be if she could have one and only one granted to her. He thought that she would ask for her eyesight to be restored, for she was blind. But to his utter amazement she quickly answered, 'One wish? Why, that I may be kept blind for the rest of my life so that the first one I shall ever see with my eyes will be Jesus.' Here was someone with her eyes fixed on Jesus . . . eyes of faith. She was blind, but she could see, and Jesus was the focus of her vision.

When William Temple, the famous Archbishop of Canterbury, was enthroned as Bishop of Manchester, he said these words to the people of his new diocese:

I come as a learner, with no policy to advocate, no plan already formed to follow. But I come with one burning desire; it is that in all our activities, sacred and secular, ecclesiastical and social,

we should help each other to fix our eyes on Jesus, making
Him our only guide . . . [2]

As we begin a new job, move house, go into a new situation,
start a new course, here is wisdom; as we begin a new ministry,
here is wisdom: we help each other to fix our eyes on Jesus.
In our churches and fellowships we can help each other or we
can hinder each other in this priority. At times we may talk
about policies and plans, visions and dreams, the way forward.
But surely William Temple's honesty has clarified our key
priority. It is that our burning desire is to help each other to
fix our eyes upon Jesus. He is the one who will inspire and
motivate us. His love compels us. We can't have a vision of
the work of the Lord if we don't have a vision of the Lord
of the work. The church is to be all about him and living out
his will in his way.

A flicker to a flame

There are times in the life of every Christian when the burning
desire is only a tiny fragile flicker. Perhaps we are tired, dis-
couraged and maybe even disillusioned. Could it be that this
is how Peter, James or John may have felt before climbing the
mountain to be with Jesus? In whatever state they went up,
they returned down to the others having caught a fresh glimpse
of Jesus Christ. They were different. They had seen what they
had never seen before and they would never be the same again.

Like Peter, James and John, we can move forward and move
on. We can be different. Through the unique ministry of the
Holy Spirit, we can hear the voice of our Father and by faith
we can see Jesus the Son. The Lord is calling us to be with
him. He calls us to look, listen, learn and lean . . . lean heavily
on him rather than live in a self-empowered mode. An iPhone
will not last long if it isn't charged. We won't last long if we

are not in touch with the one who is the source and supply of our life. We need to fix our focus on him.

Could this be the time to reassess your relationship with Jesus? If so, you might benefit from embarking on a new approach to your personal devotional life. You might consider a change in your method of Bible reading. You might explore some themes. You could use some Bible reading notes, or focus on one particular book, Gospel or epistle. You could use the prayers of others and make them your own, or write some prayers each day. Many people find support and motivation by becoming part of a prayer or Bible study group. Whatever it takes to help you focus on Christ and grow closer to him, are you willing to do it? Flames need fuel. The Christian needs Christ.

Soft knees

Sometimes, as a preacher, I am very nervous when I preach. I can think of many times when I have stood in front of a congregation with much fear and trembling. As my youngest brother-in-law said one time when I asked him how he felt when he was reading the Bible publicly in church, 'My knees were very soft!' I know the feeling. Whether young or old, we can, like Peter, learn to rely on the power of the crucified risen Christ and believe that the Lord has something to say to us and through us from his word. It is that word which is so foundational to the life and ministry of any group of God's people. To know our identity as his special people, the people of God, deepens our security in his special one. The special person Jesus has called us and he will sustain us through whatever we face. To have him in our lives at the foundation and know he is our destination gives us solid ground. To remember some of his special works in our lives and some of those special places in our lives motivates us to yearn for more.

In some church traditions, worshippers are accustomed to responding verbally at various times in church services. I first came across the following liturgical statement of faith in Singapore. It is worth learning and repeating! Each line was repeated by the congregation after the leader said it. We were encouraged to hold our Bibles and repeat as follows:

This is my Bible.
I believe this is the Word of God.
I am what it says I am.
I have what it says I have.
I can do what it says I can do.

The resources that Peter saw and received from this special person Jesus Christ are also part of the inheritance of every Christian. We are who he says we are. We have what he says we have and we can do what he says we can do. Now here are some truths which transform! Do the believers believe?

Ponder

1. Identify some of the main obstacles to you listening to God. What steps will you take to facilitate better listening?
2. What situation or which person threatens to distract you from your primary focus at this time? How will you handle that distraction?

Prayer

Lord, forgive me for not listening closely enough. Too often I do not make time to stop and hear your voice. Lord, I commit myself to being a good listener, an attentive listener, an obedient listener. Help me to look to you for my guidance and instructions, for my resources and strength. Thank you for loving me even as I am now and please help me to learn, to look, to listen and to lean more heavily on you. Lord Jesus, I want to press on to know you better. Amen.

6. What is that to you?

When Peter saw him, he asked, 'Lord, what about him?'
(John 21:21)

It is extraordinary how we can be getting on with God's business and unexpectedly we are caught off guard by a development within our own soul. It takes us by surprise because it is not usually how we are, and the thoughts are not those we regularly entertain. We see others making progress and rather than rejoicing, we are filled with envy. How often have church members prayed that the church will grow and when it does, those very same church members become part of the opposition against new people being given responsibility? In Ireland (and indeed elsewhere) we say, 'Our noses have been put out!' We pray for God's blessing on others and then when he does bless them, we cannot cope with it. Peter had that experience.

Towards the end of the breakfast on the beach, Jesus lays the cards on the table regarding Peter's future. He states categorically that the future for Peter will be a cross-shaped future. There will be suffering, and there will be pain. Peter's reaction is intriguing. Although he is on a new path, distinct hints of the old Peter break through. Remember he had jumped out of the fishing boat to run over to Jesus. He had left the boat, the nets and the other disciples. He was so glad to see the risen Jesus. His Lord was not dead. In response to the questioning of Jesus, he has expressed his loyal love. At this very time he now notices John, the beloved disciple. At that moment, something of the old Peter surfaces. The story is told in John 21:18–23. Jesus said to him:

> 'Very truly I tell you, when you were younger you dressed yourself and went where you wanted; but when you are old you will stretch out your hands, and someone else will dress you and lead you where you do not want to go.' Jesus said this to indicate the kind of death by which Peter would glorify God. Then he said to him, 'Follow me!'
>
> Peter turned and saw that the disciple whom Jesus loved was following them. (This was the one who had leaned back against Jesus at the supper and had said, 'Lord, who is going to betray you?') When Peter saw him, he asked, 'Lord, what about him?'
>
> Jesus answered, 'If I want him to remain alive until I return, what is that to you? You must follow me.' Because of this, the rumour spread among the believers that this disciple would not die. But Jesus did not say that he would not die; he only said, 'If I want him to remain alive until I return, what is that to you?'
> (John 21:18–23)

Ready to pounce

Jesus had spoken specifically to Peter about following him and what this would mean for him personally. Peter immediately began thinking about another disciple rather than taking on board the plans for his own life. We see this same pattern in all kinds of relationships. We see it in families. One child is spoken to and encouraged. Almost immediately, another child is drawing attention to himself or the first child wants to know what will happen to a brother or a sister. It happens when a relative dies and the contents of the will begin to emerge. 'What has she got? What has he got?' and 'She has been left what I wanted and I am entitled to!' can be the first questions and comments, rather than appreciation of what has been received. It is a familiar scene. We see it in churches as well. One person is watching another to see what attention they receive. Will another person be the focus of attention? Like a wild cat with attentive gaze, we are scanning the surrounding life in the church. We watch and we are ready to pounce if we see someone else attract the praise that we feel should really be ours. We look with more than usual concentration to see who will be sitting where. Who will be seated beside the minster/pastor/bishop/special guest?

We see this dynamic when one person is asked to do a particular task and another person isn't. One person is thanked and another isn't. One person is invited to play an instrument or sing in the music group or choir and another one isn't. Someone else's child is given a part in the nativity play and our child isn't. All hell can break loose. Cracks emerge in the church fellowship. One person isn't speaking to another. Families aren't speaking to one another. The issue can dominate the life of a church. A committee is formed to investigate the origins of this crisis. A special church meeting is called. How did it all start? It started just as it did with Peter! It started with a jealous thought which was expressed in a missing-the-mark question . . . what about him? What about her? And Jesus asks us, as he asked Peter, 'What is that to you?'

Follow me

Then he speaks into our soul as he did into Peter's life and soul: 'Follow me!' Discipleship is not about being rocked when others gain attention, but rather about being locked into Christ's will for us.

I wonder, many years later, did Peter have this learning curve in mind when he wrote the following?

> Therefore, rid yourselves of all malice and all deceit, hypocrisy, envy and slander of every kind . . . Dear friends, I urge you, as foreigners and exiles, to abstain from sinful desires, which wage war against your soul.
>
> (1 Peter 2:1, 11)

Peter speaks of a definite, decisive rejection of the evil thoughts and loveless words. A clear-out is needed. He advocates a thorough spring-cleaning of our hearts and an intentional, comprehensive detox of our minds. To walk the path of jealousy is to pick up more poison with every step. The footprints we leave behind are toxic, dangerous and divisive. This is a far cry from abstaining from sinful desires. In fact, it is capitulation to evil forces which seek to kill, separate and destroy. Too quickly we can become a cauldron of disunity rather than a catalyst promoting unity. Relationships are soured. Other people are devoured. God is dishonoured.

The young, good-looking and extremely gifted King Saul lost his gifting, his leadership and his very soul because of jealousy. One of the turning points in Saul's life was after the dramatic defeat of Goliath. Although impressed with the young David, he was irritated and angry at the attention David received. With dancing and singing the victory was celebrated, but with these words: 'Saul has slain his thousands and David his tens of thousands.' Significantly, the writer of Samuel comments, 'From that time on Saul kept a close eye on David' (1 Samuel 18:9).

Such a spirit of envy can invade the soul of the most talented Christian and leader. Indeed, the more we are blessed, the more alert we need to be. Our strengths and gifts can too quickly become our Achilles' heel. We lose sight of Jesus because we are envious of one of his servants. We are too caught up with self. Before we know it, we are in quicksand and we are sinking. At times we can pull others down with us. We are trapped. Peter tells us to resist the devil, who prowls around like a roaring lion, seeking whom he may devour. However, it can be his more subtle approaches which are more effective in pulling us down.

The Irish writer Oscar Wilde was well known for his story-telling. In one of his stories he tells of how the devil was once crossing the Libyan Desert. He came upon a spot where a small number of demons were tormenting a holy hermit. The sainted man easily shook off their evil suggestions. The devil watched as his lieutenants failed to sway the hermit. Then he stepped forward to give them a lesson. 'What you do is too crude,' he said. 'Permit me for one moment.' With that he whispered to the holy man, 'Your brother has just been made Bishop of Alexandria.' Suddenly a look of malignant jealousy clouded the once serene face of the holy hermit. Then the devil turned to his imps and said, 'That is the sort of thing which I should recommend.'

His distinctive work of art

Thankfully Peter resisted the evil one and listened to what Jesus was saying. Wisely he did what Jesus said and he prioritized following. He focused on Jesus rather than John. It was a real test of his newly expressed commitment to love and to follow. He didn't go down the track of the holy hermit. Peter could have lost his way at this point, but he didn't. He realized that Christ's purposes for each of us are unique and special. We have been created to be his distinctive work of art. Only we Christians can walk in his path for our lives. F. B. Meyer in his book, *Gospel of John*, expresses this same truth in a quaint but compelling way.

> The ancients thought of their lives as woven on the loom of spiteful fates, whom they endeavoured to humour by calling euphonious names. The materialist supposes that his life is the creature of circumstances, a rudderless ship in a current, mere flotsam and jetsam on the wave. The Christian knows that the path of his life has been prepared for him to walk in; and that its sphere, circumstances, and character are due to the thought and care of Him who has adapted it to our temperament and capabilities, to repress the worst, and educate the best within us.

We have been created by God for God. All things work together for good for those who love him. He has a way for us to go, a life for us to live, a road for us to travel. No-one else can walk that path for us. When we become jealously obsessed with others and God's work in their lives, we can lose the plot and miss the way in our own lives. Peter refused to give in to that temptation. He was a faithful follower. He heard the question, 'What is that to you?' He gave his answer and it was the right one. He has taught us another lesson.

Ponder

1. In which areas of your life are you most prone to jealousy?
2. When was the last time you were jealous of someone? What were the circumstances? What helped you address it?

Prayer

Lord, thank you that your teaching is clear and your purposes the best for me. Forgive me when I slip into childish behaviour and dangerous jealousy. May I be a person with a generous spirit, one who genuinely and sincerely rejoices when others are blessed. Give me the love that is in your heart and the determination to follow even when the going is tough. May I be an encourager of unity and an affirmer of others. May I be a blessing in my church and not a problem. Please help those I know who at this time are struggling with a jealous spirit and release them into freedom. Give them the wisdom to choose the path Peter chose. In the name of Jesus I pray. Amen.

Handling failure
Is there a way back up
for me when I fall?

7. The breaking can be the making

If the Bible, is about anything it is about *grace*. It is fascinating to see how popular Philip Yancey's book, *What's So Amazing About Grace?*, has been. A nerve has been touched in the Christian world. I am delighted that through reading it many have entered into a new understanding and fresh appreciation of God's grace. In the mercy-shaped eyes of a God of grace, failure and brokenness are not final. They can actually become the springboards to greater exploits in and for the kingdom of God. Peter knew all about grace, the undeserved forgiveness and favour of the Lord. In fact Peter was a grace man. He was touched, saturated, undergirded and flooded by grace.

As we have already discovered, Peter could be brash, volatile and unpredictable. His works did not always back up his words. His intentions were good, but they did not always result in appropriate action. He would speak before thinking. Publius the Greek sage once said, 'I have often regretted my speech, never my silence.' Peter knew that feeling only too well. Too often he regretted his speech. Too soon he opened his mouth. Too quickly he said too much. He didn't always live up to his extravagant claims. The classic example of this is recorded in all four Gospels. We start in Luke 22:54.

> Then seizing [Jesus], they led him away and took him into the house of the high priest. Peter followed at a distance. And when some there had kindled a fire in the middle of the courtyard and had sat down together, Peter sat down with them. A servant girl saw him seated there in the firelight. She looked closely at him and said, 'This man was with him.'
>
> But he denied it. 'Woman, I don't know him,' he said.
> (Luke 22:54–57)

In another Gospel, the writer Mark records these words:

> While Peter was below in the courtyard, one of the servant girls of the high priest came by. When she saw Peter warming himself, she looked closely at him.
>
> 'You also were with that Nazarene, Jesus,' she said.
>
> But he denied it. 'I don't know or understand what you are talking about,' he said.
> (Mark 14:66–68)

Big heart, big fall

Before we focus on Peter's failure and denial, it must be noted that, to his credit, he was the only disciple anywhere near Jesus. The others had gone, with the possible exception of John the beloved disciple. But Peter had not walked away. Peter may have had a big mouth, but he also had a big heart. Let's be fair. He did care. He was there. His desire was to be near his Lord, even though he was following at a distance. But temptation is a strange thing. Sometimes our desire is to be with Christ, to be near Christ, but our words and actions deny Christ.

It is easy to criticize Peter. But haven't you done the same? Have you not found that at a time when you have given the most, you have fallen the hardest? For many preachers, Sunday evening is one of the most dangerous times of the week. For many Christians, the moment of greatest opportunity is also the moment of greatest danger. Our area of greatest strength can also be our area of greatest weakness. Before we know it, like Peter we have denied the Lord. In a situation of pressure we have compromised. At a moment of success we have failed. The wrong decision was taken. Our whole world was shaken. We reckoned we were standing and we fell. We fell far – like Humpty Dumpty, we ended up in pieces. In the Christian story, the King himself puts us back together again.

Seen . . . heard . . . shattered

The light of the fire exposed Peter. His face could be seen. The sound of his voice with his Galilean accent was another giveaway. His distinctive accent was recognized. With protests, anger and cursing, he denied Christ. 'I don't know what you are talking about. I don't know him!' he said forcefully and angrily.

Let those words sink in. They are unbelievable. 'I don't know him!' This is heavyweight. This is hard core. This is the disciple who said he would follow Christ anywhere. This is the man who was willing to give everything for Jesus. 'I don't know him!' he shouted defiantly. It was not only a lie. It was denial and betrayal. Peter did know him. Jesus certainly knew Peter. He knew his weaknesses, his vulnerable areas. He knew him better than Peter knew himself. And then there was another sound – the rooster crowed. Dawn broke and Peter broke. He remembered what Jesus had said. His pride was shattered and his spirit broken. His life would never be the same again.

A look and a word

Was it just the sound of the rooster crowing which convicted
Peter? No, I believe it was a look and a word.

> The Lord turned and *looked* straight at Peter. Then Peter
> remembered *the word* the Lord had spoken . . .
> (Luke 22:61)

Remember, the very first time Jesus and Peter met, the Lord
had looked straight into his eyes. Now the Lord looks again.
Peter was near enough to see those penetrating eyes. And
what did Peter see in them? Rebuke? I don't think so. Did he
see that 'I told you so' look? I don't think so. Did he see condemnation? I don't think so. The Apostle Paul wrote that there
is no condemnation for those who are in Christ Jesus. So what
did Peter see? I believe he saw compassion and grace. The eyes
that had seen his potential are now filled with the moisture
of grace. Peter is overcome, and breaks. His eyes are filled
with the tears of regret, remorse and repentance. He goes
outside and weeps bitterly, deeply, intensely, profoundly. There
is no big talk now. There is no seeking to justify himself. There
are no attempts to cover up. He knows what he has done.
Peter is a broken man.

I remember being called one day to the home of a Christian
couple. The wife had just heard her husband confess to having
had an affair. He was utterly distraught and repentant. He
couldn't change what he had done but he profoundly regretted
it. I can still hear the depth and the pain of his weeping and
his uncontrollable sobbing, an utterly and totally broken man.
That was Peter. His heart was full of pain and remorse. He
had blown it. What a crisis! What a crash!

It was not just night-time when this happened. In Peter's
soul it was night . . . but piercing through all of the darkness

of the night, there was also light, the light of grace. The light shone from the eyes of Jesus. It was surprising, startling and undeserved. This is the Jesus way. The good news of the gospel is that his light still shines. His grace still flows. He still looks with mercy. His heart is still open. The river of his compassion will never dry up. The wells of his grace will never run out.

Nothing has changed

Jesus still looks into our eyes and our lives. His eyes are full of generous compassion and lavish grace. He looks at you and me. Jesus knows us better than we know ourselves. He knows those areas of our lives where we face the most subtle and persistent temptation. He sees when and where no-one else sees. He knows the deeply personal issues we are wrestling with today. He looks at our hearts and he longs to help.

Pause

1. What do you think God sees as he looks into your heart right now, today?
2. Does he see failure? Does he recognize rebellion? Is he looking at disillusionment?
3. Does he see some secret, which you know is crushing you and holding you back from moving forward with the Lord?
4. Does he see someone known as a respected Christian leader who, however, on the inside is really struggling?

The message from the life of Peter is that this same Jesus *can* help us. He can help us now. Uniquely, he can do something. The liberating truth is that we have been made to do business with God. Peter would remember another time when he had been helped and rescued by Jesus. Peter was at sea and in the sea! It was also night-time then. The disciples were in the boat and to their absolute astonishment, they saw Jesus walking on the water (Matthew 14:22–33). Peter was the only one who got out of the boat to walk to Jesus. He began walking on water until he saw the reality of the extreme weather conditions. He began to sink and cried out, 'Lord, save me!' Just as Jesus reached out his hand and caught Peter then, so that same grace is expressed now.

Perhaps we are overwhelmed at this time. In every sense it is a sinking feeling. Jesus walks towards us as he moved to help Peter. Often the real help we need is some heart surgery, or more accurately, open-heart surgery. Christ is the surgeon. Being the patient, it is not the most comfortable of themes to consider. It can be personally painful. It can be costly working through some issues but it is ultimately for our own good. Peter discovered that.

The breaking can be the making

After this, we will see a significant change in Peter's life. The next substantial conversation between Jesus and Peter is beside the Sea of Galilee when the risen Jesus meets with a Peter who repeatedly affirms and proclaims his love for Jesus. There is no self-justification, but rather a commitment to follow. His breaking point was a turning point. A new Peter emerges, a humble, teachable and more open Peter . . . a Peter willing to change and be changed. Now here is a key to spiritual growth and effectiveness . . . this willingness to change and be changed. When breaking happens for us, God is doing something deep within us. Though it's painful, in the purposes of God a breaking is positive.

Psalm 51 is a psalm which illustrates this same dynamic. David is a heartbroken man. He has committed adultery with Bathsheba. He has slept with another man's wife and cruelly

despatched the husband to his death. He sees all too painfully
that he has harmed and hurt those closest to him. He has
betrayed trust. He has let himself down and disobeyed God.
He cries out for mercy and longs to be clean. He appeals to
the Lord's unfailing love. He realizes the depth of the horror
of his attitudes and actions, and that primarily sin is something
against God. It is utterly offensive to God. David prays for a
new heart and a faithful, steadfast spirit.

> Have mercy on me, O God,
>   according to your unfailing love;
> according to your great compassion
>   blot out my transgressions.
> Wash away all my iniquity
>   and cleanse me from my sin . . .
> Against you, you only, have I sinned
>   and done what is evil in your sight . . .
> Cleanse me with hyssop, and I will be clean;
>   wash me, and I will be whiter than snow . . .
> Create in me a pure heart, O God,
>   and renew a steadfast spirit within me.
> (Psalm 51:1–2, 4, 7, 10)

The magnificent mystery of the gospel is that sin can be
forgiven, the dirt can be removed and the guilty can be released.
Failure is not final. The breaking of a person can be the making
of them. Out of death can come life. New seeds can be planted.
New shoots can grow. New life can flourish. This is the resurrection hope Peter writes about:

> Praise be to the God and Father of our Lord Jesus Christ! In
> his great mercy he has given us new birth into a living hope
> through the resurrection of Jesus Christ from the dead, and

into an inheritance that can never perish, spoil or fade. This inheritance is kept in heaven for you, who through faith are shielded by God's power until the coming of the salvation that is ready to be revealed in the last time. In all this you greatly rejoice, though now for a little while you may have had to suffer grief in all kinds of trials. These have come so that the proven genuineness of your faith – of greater worth than gold, which perishes even though refined by fire – may result in praise, glory and honour when Jesus Christ is revealed.
(1 Peter 1:3–7)

Some years ago I went through a time that was intensely painful. It was like a dying but also in the dying something was birthed. Jesus said that unless the kernel of wheat falls into the ground and dies, it remains only a single seed. But if it dies, it produces many seeds. I discovered that in the kingdom of God, a metaphorical dying is good for you. It certainly was in my life as I experienced a dying of anything that was going to hold me back from going God's way. It was a dying of some disappointments with God. It was a dying of being more concerned with what others thought than with what God thought. It was a dying of being satisfied with less than the best.

This time was one of those defining moments in my life, when once again I surrendered all to the Lord. I knew the Lord was doing something very deep within me. A few weeks after that experience of God, I was elected Bishop and I have inscribed on the inside of my bishop's ring that text from John 12:24 where Jesus speaks of the seed falling into the ground and dying. I never want to forget that with Christ, dying and giving birth are part of the same process. There is hope in the pain. Our breaking is our making. It is for his glory. It is for our good.

Ponder

1. How do you deal with failure in your own life – and in the lives of others?
2. How can you be more effective in helping the wounded and loving the broken, as well as dealing with the healthy?
3. Do you need to talk with some trusted Christian friend about issues of sin and brokenness in your own life? Who? When? Don't delay!

Prayer

Thank you, Lord, for your endless patience and limitless love. Thank you for the rivers of grace which have flowed into my heart and life. Thank you for your waves of forgiveness and streams of mercy. You are the God of a fresh start and thank you that in you, failure is not final. There is a way through and a way on. Help me to be a grace giver. Enable me to be a blessing in the lives of my family and the people I know. Use me to help the wounded and be an encourager of the broken-hearted. May I be a channel of hope to those who have failed. Lord, from the bottom of my heart I thank you for your look of love and your gift of grace. Amen.

8. Forgiven and forgiving

Forgive us our debts, as we have also forgiven our debtors.
(Matthew 6:12)

Love one another deeply, from the heart.
(1 Peter 1:22)

Finally, all of you . . . love one another, be compassionate and
humble. Do not repay evil with evil or insult with insult. On
the contrary, repay evil with blessing, because to this you were
called so that you may inherit a blessing.
(1 Peter 3:8–9)

The church of Christ is full of failed people . . . who have
been forgiven. The Lord has chosen the weak, the vulnerable
and the sinful. The story of the people of God is a story of
failure and grace, of frailty and faith. Abraham, the friend
of God, failed. David, the man after God's own heart, failed.
Peter failed, but where sin abounds, much more does grace
abound. The love of Christ is generous and abundant.
Followers of Christ are called to be the same – generous

in mercy, abundant in grace, loving one another as Christ loves us.

What is our attitude towards others when they fail and fall? We can display glaring gaps in grace when a fellow Christian has a moral collapse, makes a mighty mistake or behaves dishonourably. Instead of being a grace-filled community, too often we are graceless, standing in judgment on those whose mistakes have become painfully public. In contrast to Jesus, we seem to understand failure as final. Instead of working towards redemption, repentance and restoration, we become judge and jury. Mercy can be minimal. Love absent. Law reigns.

Sometimes we are too selective. We 'think' we know who will make it into God's arms and who will grow in the kingdom of God. Too quickly we become like the Pharisees . . . tight, legalistic and pedantic . . . missing the mark entirely. To make things even worse, we can sometimes be heartless with people when they are heartbroken. We dispel a 'Peter' with rejection rather than lead them into restoration. When those things happen, we have ceased to walk in the footsteps of Jesus.

Christ-shaped grace

Of course we must take sin seriously. Of course discipline in the church is necessary. Of course repentance is foundational . . . but repentance is devalued if it doesn't meet with forgiveness. The Lord's mercy is often wider than ours. The prodigal son's journey home is a wasted journey if a big-hearted father is not there to meet him. He may as well have stayed in the pigsty eating with the pigs. Again and again, Peter found in Jesus the big heart of astonishing and astounding grace. It was miraculous and marvellous mercy. Such divine generosity changed Peter's life. This quality and expression of Christ-shaped grace changes lives today.

As the famous hymn writer Frederick Faber expresses so powerfully:

There's a wideness in God's mercy,
Like the wideness of the sea;
There's a kindness in His justice,
Which is more than liberty.
But we make His love too narrow
By false limits of our own;
And we magnify His strictness
With a zeal He will not own.

The Lord draws in those we drive out. He reaches out to those we have pushed away. Jesus mixed with the prostitutes and the poor, the empty and lost – and he still does today! Some don't like it. They keep their respectable distance. The hypocrites huff, the arrogant puff . . . and Jesus blows their loveless house down. He will have none of it because with him, there is a way back. He is the Saviour. As always, Christ is full of surprises! Peter knows it and he reaches out and receives.

Forgiveness like Christ's

One of the outstanding leaders in the twentieth-century church was Dr Billy Graham. A well-known evangelist in the USA became a public disgrace because of scandal which involved sex, money and dodgy business transactions. He was charged, convicted and imprisoned. In a grace-filled way and with numerous acts of generosity, Billy and Ruth Graham maintained a friendship with this man throughout his imprisonment and afterwards. They had him to their cabin for dinner. They even sat beside him, publicly, in church. The fallen leader was deeply humbled and overwhelmed by the Christ-like goodness and grace of the Grahams. He had behaved like Peter. They behaved like Jesus.

A way back

All leaders know that there are times when those we lead will get things horribly wrong. If God welcomes a sinner home, surely his church can do the same. One of the first choruses I learned as a child I have never forgotten.

> There's a way back to God from the dark paths of sin.
> There's a door that is open and you may go in.
> At Calvary's cross is where you begin.
> When you come as a sinner to Jesus.
> (E. H. Swinstead)

Christ doesn't view failure as a terminal illness. In him there is a way back. Through the forgiveness and strength of Jesus we can move forward. We need to absorb that truth for others – and for ourselves.

Fall down . . . and get up again

My favourite football team is Manchester United. I remember around the time when the club was showing interest in a talented young Dutch player called Ruud van Nistelrooy, the front page of *The Times* newspaper carried a photograph showing the player lying on the ground clutching his leg. He had been approached by Manchester United and was just about to be signed as a member of the club when disaster struck. He was injured in training and finished up in hospital. Potentially the deal would be either delayed or called off. The player was faced with a choice. He could give in and give up, or he could face the challenge, and learn from it. He could move on – and this was the route he chose. Later he was signed up by Manchester United and became an important player on a very successful team.

The athlete Eric Liddell did the same. His story was told in the popular film *Chariots of Fire*. He was in a very important race but during the race he fell. In the film, the camera zoomed in on him. It is a powerful moment, a decisive moment. What will he do? Will he stay down or get up? He gets up, starts running and wins the race.

Peter did exactly the same. He fell but he got up and started running again. The heartfelt tears turned to deeper trust. The man of God emerged from the forgiving waters of God's grace. We all have choices to make. In one sense, holiness is a choice. Repentance is a choice. Moving forward and going deeper with God is a choice. On the shore of the Sea of Galilee, Peter heard again a call from the lips of the Jesus he loved. It was a call to discipleship: 'Follow me' (John 21:19). Peter could have chosen not to follow. He could have chosen to walk out on the disciples at this point. He could have chosen to forsake Christ permanently . . . but he didn't. He chose to go on. Go, baptize, make disciples and teach. This is what Jesus had called him to do. Those are the very things Peter went on to do. The Christian life is, and will be, full of challenge and difficulty; this is what Jesus promised. Peter knew all about it. He who endures to the end will be saved.

Our responses matter

The disturbing reality is that there are times when we all get it wrong and we get it all wrong. We sin, we fail, we fall. What do we do? It is easy to blame others. It is convenient to shift responsibility. Adam and Eve did the same. However, the bottom line is that we have a choice to make.

Compare two stories from Northern Ireland, the part of

the world where I come from, and a place that has seen so much pain.

A Loyalist murderer was jailed, but while in prison he changed. Though he repented of killing someone who had once been his friend, he never managed properly to get back up again after this great fall. In an interview, he said he never felt he was a whole person again. He lost something on that day, something that he never got back. Tragically, he hanged himself in September 1998, six months after the Good Friday Agreement. His suicide note read: 'I was a victim too. Please let our next generation live normal lives. Tell them of our mistakes and admit to them our regrets. I've decided to bring this to an end now. I'm tired.'

Contrast the pain and heartbreak of this death with that of a young keen Christian student at Queen's University in Belfast. As she was leaving her church one day in east Belfast, a terrorist gunman opened fire. Although completely innocent she was shot and admitted to the Royal Victoria Hospital in Belfast, critically ill. As she lay dying, with her family around her bed, they heard her trying to sing the words of a Christian chorus: 'I will enter His gates with thanksgiving in my heart, I will enter His courts with praise.' She entered glory singing. Death was defeated. Christ was honoured. Even in this situation of tragedy, heartbreak and apparent failure, the faith of a young girl in the grace of Christ was strong and radiant. Nothing can separate the Christian from the love of Christ. She kept going.

Heartbeat

In Christ, there is always more and there is always hope. We can start walking again and living again. This lesson, learned in such a dramatic way by Peter, should be part of the very heartbeat of the church. The lesson is simple but life-transforming. In Christ, failure is not final. There is hope in a hurting world. We can get going again. This is our message to a world where so many feel utterly hopeless and have concluded that there's no point in going on.

Peter kept going. He was forgiven and wonderfully reinstated by Jesus. By the grace of God you and I can keep going . . . for Christ keeps us, his hold is strong and even in our failures, he will not let us go! In him and through him there is forgiveness. Peter knew someone who loved him from the heart. Such love made all the difference, because it was forgiving, releasing and rainbow-coloured. We are to love with that kind of love. As we do, more Peters will find hope in him who is the source and ground of our hope. We may lose some battles, but Christ has won the war! Praise him!

Ponder

1. Is there someone to whom you need to say sorry?
2. Is there someone who has hurt you and to whom you need to exercise forgiveness?
3. Is there a broken, soured or difficult relationship in which you need to make the first move towards reconciliation?

Prayer

Thank you, Lord, for your amazing forgiveness. Thank you that there is a wideness in your mercy and a way back from failure and sin. Thank you for welcoming me home where I truly belong. Please help me to be more compassionate towards all who fail. Help me to reach out to others as you have reached out to me. Forgive me that too often I am more like the elder brother than the forgiving father. Please help me to be a person with a big heart and open welcoming arms. Lord Jesus, may we forgive the trespasses of others as you have forgiven ours. Amen.

Forward into God's future
What will my life as
an authentic leader
look like?

9. Do you love me?

What is to motivate the church to Christ-like living and daring discipleship? What prompts the people of God to be faithful servants of Christ the King? If Peter is to feed the sheep and take care of them, what will inspire him to do just that? Let us think back to the breakfast on the beach (John 21:15–17), mentioned at the start of Chapter 3 in this book. Three times Jesus asks Peter, 'Do you love me?'

Some commentators suggest that Peter's three-fold denial is now countered by a three-fold opportunity to renew his commitment to Christ. Christ asks, 'Do you love me more than these?' (John 21:15). Others think that Jesus was referring to the fisherman's nets lying in the boat or on the shore. In other words, did he love Christ more than he loved his work, his business? Was Jesus asking if Peter loved him more than the other disciples? Did Peter love him more than he loved other people? Whatever the precise meaning of the questions, it is with rugged conviction that Peter declares from the depths of his heart, 'Lord, you know all things; you know that I love you.' Whatever the subtleties of the questioning and the conversation, one thing is sure. Peter really loves Christ.

His love is not just an emotional response; it is a deep heart and life commitment. He has been tested in the fire. Now he is in no doubt whatsoever that he loves Christ more than anyone or anything else. I believe that Peter's responses are evidence of one of the most significant points and defining moments in his life. His colours are nailed to the mast. His goal in life is fixed. His uncertainties are resolved, his heart is focused. He really has left his nets. He *loves* Christ the Son of the living God. Christ will be the first in his heart.

At the heart of ministry is the ministry of the heart

Isn't it interesting that of all the questions Jesus could have asked, he asks this one – 'Do you love me?' Ministry is a call to love. It is a call from the Lord *of* love. It is a response of love. Love is an essential condition of Christian service. Of course the mind is important. Of course training is essential. Of course teaching is helpful. But we can have a brilliant mind, extensive training, hands laid on us by pastors, elders, bishops and even archbishops, but if our hearts do not love him, we are empty vessels. We are clanging cymbals (1 Corinthians 13:1). We can be Christian professionals and have the form of ministry. But if our hearts are not on fire with love for Christ, he cannot use us. I know, because I have been there. I was a Christian professional saying the right things, but my heart had grown cold. I was wearing the dog collar. I was in ordained ministry. I was doing the right things, saying the right words and going to the right places, but something vital was missing.

This is what happened to the church in Ephesus. The outward appearances were such that many would have considered it the church to which they should belong. There was so much in the church in Ephesus that was good and right. This was a church with a superb reputation. The people in the church were busy and active. The annual report would have been positive, indeed glowing. Yet Jesus had to say to his people in this church in the great city of Ephesus, 'I hold this against you: you have forsaken your first love' (Revelation 2:4). This was devastating. How those Christians saw the church and how Jesus saw the church were quite different.

This can happen today. In a church, or any Christian movement, the same dynamic can occur. The reality, in contrast to the reputation, is that we can lose our first love. It can happen not only in the lives of others, but in our own lives. The real issue is not a different programme or another course. It is a heart issue. Do we really, *really* love Jesus? On the beach, Peter was affirming that his first love and loyalty was Jesus. He did love him. The fisherman was a follower of the carpenter and nothing would deter him from that commitment. He was decisive, intentional and determined. He would follow Jesus and he did. Once again we can learn from Peter.

A deep inner threat
Henri Nouwen is a famous Roman Catholic priest and the author of many books. When he was in his fifties, he found himself burnt out. He went through a period of soul-searching at this time of his life. Having spent twenty years of his ministry at Notre Dame University, Yale and Harvard, he became uneasy, restless and concerned about his personal walk with God. The pilgrimage God had led him through was a most unusual one. He has recorded the journey in his book, *In The Name of Jesus*. He writes with disarming and refreshing candour. What he shares penetrates so deeply, we may find ourselves convicted to the core. After twenty years in the academic world as a teacher of Pastoral Psychology, Pastoral Theology and Christian Spirituality, Henri Nouwen reveals:

I began to experience a deep inner threat. As I entered into my
fifties and was able to realize the unlikelihood of doubling
my years, I came face to face with the simple question . . .
Did becoming older bring me closer to Jesus?[1]

What a question! It's a heart question. How would you answer
it? What is your response? Are you growing closer and
stronger?

That is the reality Peter had to face up to. Did he really love
Jesus and was he growing closer to him? Again I ask . . . what
about you? It is my experience that as some people grow
older, they become more disgruntled and more destructively
critical. They become more and more selfish in their ways,
and alarmingly mean in their attitudes. They are like a
grumbling appendix in the Body of Christ. They are trouble-
some to their friends and an annoyance to their neighbours.
Unsurprisingly and consistently they cause trouble. Christ's
call is to love him, and love him to the end. Peter was now
absorbing this truth into his mind and heart. Loving Christ
means loving others.

Isn't she beautiful?

Some years ago my aunt, who was really like a mother to me,
was dying of Alzheimer's disease. For many years her husband
had cared for her at home sacrificially and adoringly. Eventually
she had to be admitted into residential care. Just hours
before she died, I was sitting with my uncle at her bedside. As
we sat for a few moments in silence I looked at her. All kinds
of thoughts, emotions and memories flooded my mind. I
thought of her kindness and generosity. I thought of how good-
looking and attractive she once was. In that room in the
nursing home, I saw someone so different to the aunt I had
known all my life. She looked like an old woman. Her face

was wrinkled and tired-looking. The few teeth she had left were grinding against one another. Her eyes were sunken and her skin was pale. Her beauty had faded. She looked at least twenty years older than she was. Then my uncle broke the silence and said to me, 'Kenneth, isn't she beautiful? Look at those beautiful eyes.' And then he did something which I will never forget. He leant forward and kissed her on her lips. I was moved to tears. He adored her to the end. He was devoted, loyal and faithful. Why? Because he loved her! This bridegroom of so many years before still loved his bride. This husband loved his wife. At that moment, I saw something of Christ's love for the church. It is selfless. It is sacrificial. It is cross-shaped. There is nothing like it.

Christ loved Peter to the end and Peter knew it. There on that beach, restorative grace was flowing. Peter was being restored and released . . . released from the guilt of sin and the shame of failure. Forgiveness was expressed graciously, firmly, generously . . . and he knew it. There was more than the light of the early morning sun shining that morning on the beautiful shores of the Sea of Galilee. The light was also dawning in Peter's mind, heart and soul. He was being trusted and entrusted with a task. Christ had called him not only to be a fisher of men but also to be a shepherd in the church of God. Peter was accepted. He was forgiven and reinstated. He was back on track. This would be a day he would never forget . . . another one!

The preaching and the preacher

One of the best encouragers I have ever known was a preacher and Bible teacher called Canon Harry Sutton. I have often said that Harry Sutton could have enthused a corpse! At one point in his ministry, unexpectedly, he developed a serious throat problem. A growth was discovered on his vocal chords.

Within forty-eight hours he was admitted into Guy's Hospital in London. He was informed by the doctor, 'It may be that after this operation you will never be able to speak naturally again.' For a preacher, few things are more devastating than hearing news like that. Harry had his operation and for fourteen weeks afterwards, he couldn't utter a word. It appeared that his ministry was at an end. He had to write down all his words on a little writing tablet. Around this time, on his own admission, he was mildly depressed. One day in his back garden, sitting beside his wife, he wrote on his tablet, 'Olive, I'm going to pray this prayer: will you kneel down and pray it with me?'

> Heavenly Father, for over 50 years You have had my preaching. It now looks like You're not going to have it anymore. But I'm happy to tell You that You've now got the preacher. And if I can glorify You in my silence as eloquently as I've tried to do with my noise I'll be greatly honoured.

What a prayer! What a surrender! It was similar for Peter. After this lakeside experience, Peter was unreservedly Christ's. Christ had the teacher as well as the teaching. Peter's heart was captured and captivated. His will was surrendered. His love was for Christ. Christ knew him, loved him and showed him breathtaking grace. Is it surprising that many years later, Peter would write to young Christians?

> But grow in the grace and knowledge of our Lord and Saviour Jesus Christ. To him be glory both now and forever! Amen.
> (2 Peter 3:18)

What a tragedy if, after spending this time reflecting on Peter's life and love, we were to stay the same and still hold back from a wholehearted and unreserved commitment to Christ who calls us to himself. It is relatively easy to sing worship songs of surrender. We can stand with our arms in the air and express the total self-giving of ourselves. The real challenge is to live those words we sing. From now on, Peter began to do that in a new way. He was a changed and changing Peter. He was a surrendered Peter. He loved, really loved Jesus. That's where movement forward starts. That's the spring from which new life flows. As the waters of the Sea of Galilee washed over the shore that morning, so Christ's living waters refreshed and replenished a repentant Peter. Those same waters can refresh and revive us. They flow into repentant, hungry hearts. They revitalize tired bodies. They flow into the cracks and fissures of our broken lives. They energize the weary. They rejuvenate a sagging saint. Now there's an amazing truth! The truth of Christ set Peter free. His truth still sets us free.

Ponder

1. Does the Lord have you today? Does he have all of you?
2. Are there nets which you are refusing to let go?
3. Are there some habits or attitudes which you know are choking you?

Prayer

Spend a few moments reflecting on the question Jesus asks: 'Do you love me?'

Then prayerfully meditate on the following truths.

Why would you ever complain, O Jacob,
    or, whine, Israel, saying,
'God has lost track of me.
    He doesn't care what happens to me'?

Don't you know anything? Haven't you been listening?
God doesn't come and go. God lasts.
   He's Creator of all you can see or imagine.
He doesn't get tired out, doesn't pause to catch his breath.
   And he knows everything, inside and out.
He energizes those who get tired,
   gives fresh strength to dropouts.
For even young people tire and drop out,
   young folk in their prime stumble and fall.
But those who wait upon God get fresh strength.
   They spread their wings and soar like eagles,
They run and don't get tired,
   they walk and don't lag behind.
(Isaiah 40:27–31, *The Message*)

10. Pride and prejudice

Where is God?

The fictional story is told of a vicar who posed the question to a young boy, 'Where is God?' The response was silence. The young boy neither moved nor spoke. A second time the vicar asked, 'Where is God?' Same response – silence. Impatient for a reply, the vicar posed the question a third time, in a stern voice: 'Where is God?' At this point the young boy stood up, and ran home as fast as he could.

On reaching home the boy shouted to his father, 'Daddy, Daddy, they've lost God down at the church and now they are blaming *me* for that!'

Poor lad! But it's a good question. People look at the years of violence in Northern Ireland between groups of religious people and ask, 'Where is God?' People look at the atrocities in Rwanda, Congo, Cambodia, Iraq and Afghanistan, and ask, 'Where is God?' People look at the inconsistency and lack of integrity in the lives of Christians and Christian leaders, and ask, 'Where is God?' The reports containing harrowing and horrific stories of clerical abuse of little children and young teenagers have prompted many to ask, 'Where is God?'

People look out across the world at the many ethnic groups, the plethora of faiths and the various expressions of religious experience, and they ask themselves, 'Where is God?'

The truth is that sometimes we cannot fully answer that question. At other times the answer is that the Lord is found in the most unexpected of places. That was Peter's experience and it shook him to the core. He discovered the Lord where he never expected to find him. It shocked Peter to the very depth of his being. His mind was blown, his myths exploded and his presumptions shattered.

A God of surprises

God doesn't always do the expected thing. He breaks out and does things his way. How inconvenient when he doesn't 'toe the party line'. How embarrassing when he doesn't abide by the club rules! My experience is that the Lord continually stretches and disturbs us. How alarming when the Lord doesn't conform neatly and tidily to our rigidly defined systematic theology. That was certainly Peter's experience. As we look at the life of Peter, we see that he was constantly on a learning curve. In this chapter we look at another time in his life when his vision was enlarged, his mind was stretched and his prejudices were challenged to their very roots. Neither Peter nor his ministry would ever be the same again. In many ways this is the story of the Acts of the Apostles – God doing things his way. God is breaking out of a perceived cultural and religious box. One Bible translator, J. B. Phillips, wrote in his Preface to his translation of the Acts of the Apostles:

> It is impossible to spend several months in close study of the remarkable short book, conventionally known as the Acts of the Apostles, without being profoundly stirred and, to be honest, disturbed. The reader is stirred because he is seeing

Christianity, the real thing, in action for the first time in human history. The new-born Church, as vulnerable as any human child, having neither money and influence nor power in the ordinary sense, is setting forth joyfully and courageously to win the pagan world for God through Christ. Yet we cannot help feeling disturbed as well as moved, for this surely is the Church as it was meant to be. It is vigorous and flexible, for these are the days before it ever became fat and short of breath through prosperity, or muscle-bound by over organization.

In many ways, the story of the Acts of the Apostles can be compared to ripples going out after a stone is dropped in a pond and they reach the edges. Jesus commissioned the disciples: 'You will be my witnesses in Jerusalem, and in all Judea and Samaria, and to the ends of the earth' (Acts 1:8). That's the movement and dynamic which unfolds as the book progresses. There is an explosion and expansion of the church across racial, religious, cultural and political barriers. Peter is caught up in this new movement. He doesn't carry out 'acts of faith', he simply believes. He preaches to thousands. He heals the sick. The man is on fire. In Acts 9 we read of Peter being used by the Lord in healing. In Acts 10 his mind is blown and his prejudices smashed as he takes a revolutionary step in the history of the church. I call this part of his life the 'X Factor' or more specifically the 'Cornelius Factor'. Peter discovered new horizons in God's vision and new expressions of God's grace. William Barclay refers to this tenth chapter of Acts as one of the great turning points in the history of the church.

The Cornelius factor

The story begins in the Acts of the Apostles chapter 10 at verse 1:

> At Caesarea there was a man named Cornelius, a centurion in
> what was known as the Italian Regiment. He and all his family
> were devout and God-fearing; he gave generously to those in
> need and prayed to God regularly.
> (Acts 10:1–2)

Cornelius was a leader. He was religious, generous and
prayerful. Understandably he was startled and fearful when
one day at about three in the afternoon he had a vision.

> He distinctly saw an angel of God, who came to him and said,
> 'Cornelius!'
> Cornelius stared at him in fear. 'What is it, Lord?' he asked.
> (Acts 10:3–4)

I sometimes wonder what I might have replied, if I hadn't first
fainted! The instructions were specific.

> The angel answered, 'Your prayers and gifts to the poor have
> come up as a memorial offering before God. Now send men to
> Joppa to bring back a man named Simon who is called Peter.
> He is staying with Simon the tanner, whose house is by the sea.'
> (Acts 10:4–6)

Cornelius knew what it was to receive and obey orders from
a higher authority. He was someone who knew about respect
for authority and so he acted immediately.

> When the angel who spoke to him had gone, Cornelius called
> two of his servants and a devout soldier who was one of his
> attendants. He told them everything that had happened and
> sent them to Joppa.
> (Acts 10:7–8)

It is so obvious that Cornelius was a quality person, deeply spiritual and open to God.

However, what we need to remember above all else – and this is so crucial in understanding the real thrust of this story – is that he was a *Gentile*. He was not a Jew. Because he was a Gentile, he was not on Peter's religious radar screen. In the mind of Peter and in the mindset of his family tradition, Cornelius, like all Gentiles, was an outsider.

It may well be hard for people today to comprehend the deep divide between Jews and Gentiles at that time. It was a yawning chasm. There was a great gulf fixed. Racial and religious discrimination existed in the extreme. The strict Jew believed that God had no time, nor use, for the Gentiles. The Gentiles were 'dogs'. Sometimes the strict Jew even went to the length of saying that help must not be given to a Gentile woman in childbirth because that would only be to bring another Gentile into the world. Jews and Gentiles were solar systems apart! Can you begin to imagine the reaction of someone like Peter, a strict Jew, to any suggestion of personal contact with this man or any other Gentile? It would be like asking sworn enemies to take afternoon tea together. Yet the Lord speaks to Peter in the most dramatic of ways.

The pork challenge

The story is as follows. The day after Cornelius's vision, Peter is praying. He falls into a trance. He has a vision . . . and what a vision! Something like a huge blanket was lowered down, by its four corners, from heaven to earth. It contained all kinds of animals, reptiles and birds. It was a kind of flying zoo-logical garden. A voice instructed Peter to kill and eat. But to the religious Jew, this was anathema. They adhered to very strict food laws. Some of this food didn't meet the criteria. It wasn't kosher. Peter protests, 'But I've never eaten anything impure or ritually unclean in my life.' The contrast is striking. Cornelius the outsider is open to God. Peter the religious Jew, the apostle, is (at best) cautious and hesitant. At worst he is closed to God's revelation. Peter has come a long way in his breaking of barriers, but this is one step too far. His religious prejudice is deeply ingrained in his psyche and in his thinking. He can't break free from his past.

Then the voice came a second and a third time: 'If God says it is OK, it is OK.' Events then move quickly. As Peter is reflecting on what he has seen and heard, there are two visitations – the delegation from Cornelius and the visitation from the Holy Spirit. The Holy Spirit speaks directly and specifically into Peter's mind and situation. 'Three men are looking for you. So get up and go downstairs. Do not hesitate to go with them, for I have sent them' (Acts 10:19–20). Peter meets them at the door, reveals his identity and invites them in for the night. This is a revolutionary hand of hospitality extended by Peter.

In the Jewish tradition, hospitality is an important practice, but not so far as to welcome Gentiles. Hospitality is an important ministry. It can be thoroughly enriching, though sometimes it is stretching. I love the definition of hospitality as being 'the gift of making people feel at home when you wish they were!' I have a wonderfully encouraging brother-in-law who sometimes says to us as we leave his house, 'Come back and see us when you have less time!' Such an interpretation and expression of hospitality is stretching. This encounter was stretching for Peter. It was new territory. He is entering a new dimension of experience and understanding.

Prejudice busting
Peter's welcome and invitation are groundbreaking. In his invitation to these people we see Peter engaging in some

prejudice busting. No orthodox Jew would ever enter the home of a Gentile or invite a Gentile into his home. No pious Jew would have sat down at the same table as a Gentile. Peter is giving a night's lodging to uncircum-cised Gentiles. Now, here's a development. He's moving! He's opening up! He's changing! New horizons are now being explored. New paths are being travelled. New bridges are being crossed.

The church is a company of God's people of every race, class, colour, tribe and tongue. It is national and international. It is across the nations and generations. Walls of hostility and division are broken down in Christ. Those who have historically been racially and socially divided can be one in Christ. Indeed, great power is released when God's people come together in Christ-inspired unity and authentic fellowship. Through the cross, sins are forgiven. At the cross, the ground is level. Christian people are one in Christ Jesus.

Peter was taking small steps into a new appreciation of how God works and where he is to be found. I wonder if God is leading us into new discoveries of his grace and mercy. Have you been too narrow in your understanding? Is your God too small? Are you calling impure what God has made clean? Do you honestly believe that 'everyone who believes in him receives forgiveness of sins through his name?' (Acts 10:43). Is he leading you to meet with others from whom you have kept a distance? Is he at work where you have presumed he isn't? Is it time for you really to listen to some people from whom you have been separated? It just may be that, like Peter, you have something to learn.

In the lives of many Christian leaders, we experience divine surprises. I was moved when I read these words by one of the greatest Christian leaders of the twentieth century, Dr Billy Graham. His horizons were broadened as follows:

I am now aware that the family of God contains people of various ethnological, cultural, class, and denominational differences . . . Within the true church there is a mysterious unity that overrides all divisive factors. In groups which in my ignorant piousness I formerly 'frowned upon', I have found men so dedicated to Christ and so in love with the truth that I have felt unworthy in their presence. I have learned that although Christians do not always agree, they can disagree agreeably, and that what is most needed in the church today is for us to show an unbelieving world that we love one another.[1]

Ponder

1. Is God calling you to do some prejudice busting? Who is your Cornelius?
2. Is God leading you into some new dimension of understanding? Is anything holding you back?
3. Is God leading your church or fellowship into a more biblical understanding of his nature and his ways? What will you do about it?

Prayer

Thank you, Lord, for Peter's willingness to follow you, even when you led him in a totally new direction. Thank you for Peter's courage to be led out of his comfort zone. Lord, give me that same openness to your will. Give me the courage to go where you are leading. Broaden my horizons. Lessen my prejudices. I want to follow where you lead. Lord, I accept your surprises. Amen.

11. The priority of obedience

But God has shown me . . . (Acts 10:28)
It is naive to think that life in the early church was a constant, consistent cocktail of harmony, sweetness and light. Some preachers love to give that impression. 'The early church was the ideal church. It was sin-proof and problem free.' Such a viewpoint reveals a blinkered reading of the New Testament. The first Christians regularly wrestled with issues of race and racism, religious intolerance, loveless discrimination and community division. God challenged their deep-seated prejudices and narrow vision. The story in Acts 10 is actually the story of two conversions, the conversion of the Gentile Cornelius and the conversion of the Apostle Peter's bigotry into openness. He says to Cornelius and the gathered assembly: 'You are well aware that it is against our law for a Jew to associate with or visit a Gentile. But God has shown me that I should not call anyone impure or unclean (Acts 10:28).

What a testimony! Peter's horizons have been broadened. We see an obedient Peter. For me this is another of the key turning points in the story of Peter. He was willing to go where he had never gone before and only because it was in response to the Lord's word. Like a first-century Buzz Lightyear, he went to his infinity and beyond! It may have been cautiously, apprehensively, nervously, reluctantly – we don't know precisely. However, what we do know is that he *went*! The bottom line is he *obeyed*. The next day Peter heads off with these men to visit Cornelius. One step for Peter . . . a giant step for the future of the church. This really is a most significant turning point. It is pivotal, and hinges on Peter doing what he is told.

Key to growth

In recent years I wonder if we have seen, in Christian teaching and preaching, a dilution of the principle of obedience. With so much emphasis on feelings and moods, I wonder if we have neglected the priority of just doing as we are told? It is the key to spiritual growth and lasting effectiveness. David Yonggi Cho, the Korean pastor of the largest single congregation in the world, was once asked the secret of the phenomenal growth of the church. I suspect the interviewer was waiting for the revelation of some new church growth programme or some attractive new course with ten easy steps. Yonggi Cho's answer was disarmingly simple. He replied, 'I pray a lot and I obey a lot!' Prayer and obedience are the keys which unlock so many doors. The fruit of the Spirit only grows in the garden of obedience. It is watered by prayer. The church will move forward in proportion to its levels of obedience. But it's not easy to obey.

'I don't like doing what I am told'

For many years I have admired and been greatly helped by the preaching and teaching of Stuart Briscoe. He tells an amusing story of a fishing trip with his young grandsons, Danny and

Mike. It illustrates superbly the difficulty we have in learning obedience.

On the fishing trip, the boys threw in their lines. They had the whole lake to fish in, but they decided to fish in the same square yard of water. Stuart said, 'Don't do that boys, your lines will tangle.' 'No, they won't,' was the determined reply.

Sure enough, their lines started to drift towards one another and Stuart said, 'Your lines are going to tangle.' 'No they won't!' one little grandson replied defiantly. So Stuart took authority and said, 'Danny, move!' 'But I was here first,' Danny said. Stuart responded, 'Danny, then you move first!' Danny was not a happy camper. He glared at his grandad. He reeled in his line, gave his grandad another black look and stomped across to the other side of the jetty. Still glaring, he hurled his line into the water. The hook had hardly touched the water when a fish took it and Danny shouted, 'I've got a bite, Papa. I've got a bite, Papa!' Stuart said, 'Bring it in.' As it was coming in, Danny looked over his shoulder at his grandad and said, 'You're a bit like Jesus, aren't you?' So putting on his clothes of humility Stuart said nonchalantly, 'Yeah,' and then asked, 'Why do you say that, Danny?'

His grandson said, 'Well, Peter was fishing with Jesus one day. He didn't catch anything, so Jesus told him to cast over to the other side. He did and he caught something. You know, I'm a bit like Peter, Papa.' 'Why do you say that, Danny?' 'Well, Peter didn't like doing what he was told and I don't like doing what I am told either.'

Stuart said, 'Danny, do you want to know something about old Papa? I don't like doing what I'm told either.'

Very few of us like doing what we are told. However, if we are to move forward with the Lord, we have to learn obedience. Peter was learning about God's new horizons because he was willing to obey. Just imagine what would have happened if Peter had refused to go to the house of Cornelius. Think of what he would have missed. Think of what the church would have missed. His disobedience would have closed the doors of fresh blessings. Or imagine if he had given himself to lesser things and had not prioritized the true priority. Too often, leaders choose the not-so-important action or activity rather than the most important. Peter was learning that the main thing is to keep the main thing the main thing. The main thing is always to do what is in line with God's word and will. In our daily choices, we need to keep an eye out for God's leading – sometimes it is surprising. We may even entertain angels unawares.

Grow up

If Peter needed any further convincing of the breadth of God's vision, he has it in the household of Cornelius when he sees what God does in the life of this Gentile household. While Peter is still speaking, the Holy Spirit comes in power. The Gentiles speak in tongues. They praise God. They are baptized. The gift of the Holy Spirit has been given to, and received by, the Gentiles. It is unmistakeable, undeniable and once again Peter will never be the same again . . . it is another defining moment. Notice too in this encounter the marriage of the word and the Spirit – 'the Holy Spirit came on all who heard the message' (Acts 10:44). We must never divorce what the Lord has married! The word and the Spirit are dynamically connected. As we continue further into the twenty-first century in the life of the church, let us continue to hold as foundational the inextricable link between the word of God and the Spirit of God. I love that saying which I first heard many years ago from the late Canon David Watson.

All Word and no Spirit . . . we dry up!
All Spirit and no Word . . . we blow up!
Both Word and Spirit . . . we grow up!

Our vision is to see people of all nations and generations knowing the Lord and growing up in the Lord. We are committed to all peoples and cultures hearing the good news of the gospel of Christ, whether they are Jews or Gentiles, black or white, prosperous or poverty-stricken, searching or cynical. We long to see what Peter saw . . . the Lord pouring out his Spirit in abundance on the outsiders, whoever our outsiders may be. Isn't it disturbing how we all have people and groups whom we consider to be 'on the other side'? The good news of the gospel is that God loves the people on the other side. Jesus crossed to the people on the other side and we are they. This is God's vision . . . a multicultural, multiracial, multigenerational church. Human boundaries dissolve and disintegrate before the flowing lava of God's amazing grace. God's river of salvation is unstoppable. Peter witnessed this with his very eyes.

The centrality of Christ
I find Peter's message in Cornelius's house absolutely fascinating. It is a model for the church today. Christ is at the very centre of the message. The message is both broad and narrow. It is broad in understanding the scope of salvation: 'I now realize how true it is that God does not show favouritism but accepts people from every nation who fear him and do what is right.' It is narrow in identifying the means of salvation:

'Everyone who believes in Jesus Christ receives forgiveness of sins through his name.'

This issue of salvation is one of the key areas of debate and divergence in the church today. This is nothing new. It was the same in the early church. We can learn so much from Peter in this multi-faith context. He is respectful, courteous and fair in his relationships and in his dealings with others. He is persuasive in his presentation. He is crystal clear in his doctrine. He speaks of the unique Lordship of Jesus Christ, the exclusiveness of Christ as the only Saviour and he covers the core truths of Christ's life, death and resurrection. He doesn't ignore the other two great contemporary no-go areas in the Western Church: sin and judgment. One of the most important tasks before the church today is to be faithful to the gospel, the faith once and for all delivered to the saints. These are the days of pick and mix when it comes to religious belief. There is unease and dis-ease with words like 'exclusive' and 'unique'. The god of tolerance has been exalted above all others. He is worshipped frequently throughout our country and in the Western world. Christ is perceived as only one of many saviours. As Ravi Zacharias correctly and controversially observes:

> Philosophically you can believe anything, so long as you do not claim it to be true. Morally you can practice anything, so long as you do not claim it to be a 'better way'. Religiously you can hold to anything so long as you do not bring Jesus Christ into it.
>
> If a spiritual idea is Eastern, it is granted critical immunity; if Western, it is thoroughly criticized. Thus, a journalist can walk into a church and mock its carryings-on, but he or she dare not do the same if the ceremony is from the Eastern fold. Such is the mood at the end of the twentieth century.[1]

A life-and-death issue

The twenty-first century is no different. This is the atmosphere and context in which we now function as the church in the Western world. Contemporary cultural moods seem to be more important than revealed truth. Absolutes are perceived as archaic. Relativism reigns, and pluralism holds sway. These are stretching days for orthodoxy. One of the lessons we learn from Peter is to keep Christ central . . . the one who is the way and the truth and the life (John 14:6). This is a life-and-death issue. It is a liberating gospel truth. It is mere Christianity. Let's not be so broad-minded that our brains fall out. Gifts of discernment are priceless. Jesus Christ and only Jesus Christ *is* Lord of all. This is the message of all of the apostles and it is unquestionably Peter's message on the day of Pentecost, in the home of Cornelius and afterwards.

There is a legend about a man caught in the quicksand. It is no doubt a caricature, but most caricatures contain a good element of truth.

> The man was struggling in the quicksand and passing rapidly to his death. Confucius saw him and remarked, 'There is evidence that men should stay out of such places.' Buddha came and said, 'Let that life be a lesson to the rest of the world.' Mohammed commented, 'Alas, it is the will of Allah!' A Hindu said, 'Never mind, you will return to earth in another form.' But when Jesus saw him he said, 'Give me your hand, brother, and I will pull you out.'

This is Jesus – the one who rescues, saves, transforms and renews. As Peter said:

> He commanded us to preach to the people and to testify that he is the one whom God appointed as judge of the living and

the dead. All the prophets testify about him that everyone who believes in him receives forgiveness of sins through his name. (Acts 10:42–43)

Notice the emphasis on Christ. Modify, change or dilute this message, marginalize Christ and make him one among equals, and we move away from the apostolic gospel. We are unfaithful to Christ, we distort the gospel and we cease to proclaim the truth – his truth.

Gospel and culture

Another major issue raised in this story is the whole relationship between gospel, religion and culture. The religious Peter had to engage in so much unlearning before he could begin to grasp God's exciting, expansive vision. In Northern Ireland we have wrestled with an alarming mixture of Christian truths, religious traditions and political aspirations. It has been a lethal cocktail. Perhaps others can learn from the disastrous consequences of such a cocktail being unchecked and absorbed. In some instances violence, hatred and needless deaths have been fruits of a distortion of the gospel. A particular political viewpoint or aspiration can become a condition of salvation.

I remember speaking some years ago at the Christian Union in one of our largest universities in Ireland. I had been asked to speak on John 4 . . . the intriguing encounter between Jesus and the woman of Samaria. In this meeting of Jesus and this woman, we see Jesus crossing traditional, political, cultural and religious barriers. What he is doing is revolutionary and trailblazing. The disciples are shaken.

After the Christian Union meeting, a young man verbally attacked me, stating the impossibility of someone being saved if they believed in a united Ireland. He found it impossible to believe that anyone could be a true Christian and hold that belief. Some of us need a mental deliverance from equating the gospel with belief in a particular political entity. Such a viewpoint bears more resemblance to our particular tribal tradition than to the gospel of Christ.

A courageous trailblazing Peter made a momentous journey from the land of religious traditions to a land of grace, where God's gospel defines belief and behaviour. I believe that such a journey is a priority and opportunity for the church today. As we look to the future, we can be a prophetic voice in the church worldwide, seeking to constantly encourage the church in each country to distinguish gospel essentials from cultural trappings and tribal traditions. Cultural idols can be dangerous and deadly. They can distort the gospel and delude the gospel messenger. Peter experienced a freeing deliverance from some of his cultural baggage. For him, the word of God became more important than the traditions of men. I wonder from whom he had heard such teaching. Did not Jesus teach this very truth as he interacted with the religious leaders of his time? He said to the Pharisees and religious teachers, 'You have let go of the commands of God and are holding on to human traditions' (Mark 7:8).

A new community
So after these events and this conversion experience Peter has a vision, not just of a new Christian but also of a new community. He understands that God's family is bigger than his prejudiced presuppositions allowed for. His mind has been cleansed and decommissioned. In his heart the religious barriers have been smashed, the racial barricades have been dismantled and the traditional boundaries have been extended. He has a different mindset and world view. He sees a transformed community, a new society, God's true family . . .

132 | GOING FOR GROWTH

'a chosen people, a royal priesthood, a holy nation, God's special possession' (1 Peter 2:9).

Oh yes! Who first wrote those words? Wasn't it someone called Peter? He didn't forget the pork challenge, the Cornelius factor and the Caesarea experience! Perhaps he isn't such a slow learner after all! His epistles show forcefully and vividly how much he has learned and how far he has travelled in his exciting discovery of new horizons.

Ponder

1. Identify three areas where Christ is central in your life and three areas where that is a struggle. Be specific.
2. Are there areas of disobedience in your life that God is pinpointing? What are they? How will you address them?
3. What are some of the cultural trappings and traditions that you need to revisit, review and, where necessary, release?
4. Is there someone to whom God is prompting you to reach out?

Prayer

Lord, thank you for crossing to our side and living a life of steady obedience. Forgive me for my erratic obedience and disappointing disobedience. I am really sorry, Lord. Lead me forward into new areas of fruitfulness for you. I want to discover new possibilities with you. Thank you for your wonderful new community. Amen.

12. The 3G leader

But just as he who called you is holy, so be holy in all you do.
(1 Peter 1:15)

Peter was motivated to live a life of *grace, gratitude* and *generosity*. These are the 3 Gs. They are spiritual dynamite, able to blow up the hard rock of self-centred rebellion. They blast away meanness and hypocrisy. They destroy selfishness. When they explode in a community, people enter new dimensions of relationships. Peter was called to be, and he was, a 3G leader.

Grace leads to holiness

One recent newspaper headline announced the story of one of the most famous sportsmen in England courageously coming out about the sexual abuse he suffered as a young boy. Sexual abuse is always traumatic but when, as in his case, the perpetrator was a professing Christian or Christian leader, the consequences are multiple. One of these consequences can be, understandably, that some reject Christianity because of sinfulness in the life of a Christian. The reality is that they may not have rejected the gospel, but rather they have rightly rejected the selfish and wrong behaviour of professing gospel messengers. In Ireland various reports detailing child abuse perpetrated by priests, have been devastating, heart-rending and harrowing. As a Christian, one hangs one's head in shame that such things have happened within a Christian context. May God forgive us and may the innocent children, now adults, who experienced pain, abuse and indeed personal torture, know hope and healing.

I have sometimes wondered what prompts any professing Christian to behave in this way towards children. One conclusion I am certain of is this. There is a serious deficiency in their understanding of a God of grace, the nature of grace and the cost of grace. One of the great lessons of Peter's faith journey is that his experience of God's grace led him – and indeed propelled him – into new avenues of holy living. Clear thinking about God's grace leads to clean living in God's world. Peter's experience of Christ's mercy and grace nurtured Christ-like thinking which resulted in Christ-like behaviour. He exhorts and encourages others to be and do the same, and to live lives of grace and holiness. Right at the beginning of his first letter he says, 'Grace and peace be yours in abundance' (1 Peter 1:2).

His first letter concludes on the same theme as he encourages these Christians to stand fast in the true grace of God. St Paul urged the same in writing to Timothy. 'You then, my son, be strong in the grace that is in Christ Jesus' (2 Timothy 2:1).

Peter's second letter begins in a similar way as he teases out the implications of grace. He speaks about the kind of grace which will penetrate, impact and determine the kind of people we are and the kind of lives we live: 'As he who called you is holy, so be holy in all you do' (1 Peter 1:15).

He reminds them of the price paid by the man of grace. It was not cheap. The sacrifice was great. A ransom was paid – it wasn't money, but the price was very high. It was nothing less than the precious life of Christ. The cost was God's Son. The innocent died for the guilty, the pure for the impure. If anything tells us how much we are worth and how valued we are, this is it.

> For you know that it was not with perishable things such as silver or gold that you were redeemed from the empty way of life handed down to you from your ancestors, but with the precious blood of Christ, a lamb without blemish or defect.
>
> (1 Peter 1:18–19)

All of this was at the foundation of Peter's commitment and transformation. It is this same understanding and experience of God's grace which has revolutionized the lives of millions. Again and again sin has been defeated, injustice has been attacked and poverty has been alleviated, because Christ's followers have chosen to live a different way and love their neighbours with a grace-filled love. Tragically, enormous damage is done when Christians choose selfish pursuits, adopt loveless, graceless attitudes, embark on evil encounters and engage in lust-filled actions. Peter grasped the vital connection between belief and behaviour, and hence his exhortations are to be grace-shaped Christians and grace-shaped churches.

> Live such good lives among the pagans that, though they accuse you of doing wrong, they may see your good deeds and glorify God on the day he visits us.
>
> (1 Peter 2:12)

A funeral service was held for an elderly, godly Christian man, who was a regular worshipper, in a mission hall in east Belfast. His daughter-in-law, an ordained Episcopal priest in the USA, shared with the congregation her memory of the first time they had met. She had flown from the USA with her fiancée, his son, to be introduced to him. For a variety of good reasons, she had been very apprehensive about this initial encounter. There was concern that this first meeting might not go well. She was unsure of the kind of welcome she might receive. Indeed, would she be welcomed at all? Would it be a frosty conversation? As she and his son drew up in their car outside his house, the front door was open and her future father-in-law ran out to meet her. She said that she would never forget the sight at this first encounter. His arms were outstretched, his face was smiling. His words were warm and he embraced her. She said that in that moment she saw something of God the Holy Trinity, of the Father's grace-filled heart. The arms outstretched as he approached her reminded her of Christ the Son on the cross and his loving embrace spoke to her of the Holy Spirit's work in our lives. I believe she saw and experienced grace from someone who understood it and practised it. This is the kind of action we see in a 3G Christian. An experience of grace is manifested in an expression of grace.

We see unmistakeably in Peter a man who had a grasp of grace. He understood it and was overwhelmed by it. Grace leads to gratitude.

Gratitude

> Praise be to the God and Father of our Lord Jesus Christ! In his great mercy he has given us new birth into a living hope through the resurrection of Jesus Christ from the dead . . .
> In all this you greatly rejoice . . . Therefore, with minds that

are alert and fully sober, set your hope on the grace to be
brought to you when Jesus Christ is revealed at his coming.
(1 Peter 1:3, 6, 13)

An attitude of gratitude is one of the big changes we see in
Peter's life. His heart bursts with praise as he considers the
greatness of God's mercy. This has given him hope and opened
doors of opportunity for him, both personally in his own life
and in his ministry. This positive appreciation of who God is,
this releasing understanding and experience of the breadth
and depth of God's forgiveness, are indispensable marks of a
3G leader. The twenty-first century needs leaders who are
visionary, positive, joyful and grateful. The church needs to
develop disciples with thankful hearts. A grumbling 'God
squad' can quickly and rightly be denounced as a fumbling
fraud squad. Griping and sniping are not marks of grace. A
gospel person is a grateful person. Peter had moved from
one to the other. In Singapore I first heard the statement
addressed to a Christian, 'If you have joy in your heart, please
inform your face!' Cultures and countries which know too
much of depression and recession need to see informed faces!
We are 'resurrection people' who have so much to be thankful
about and thankful for.

Gratefulness to God for his great mercy is a powerful
motivation to steady, consistent and sacrificial service. St Paul
talked about the love of Christ controlling us. He could never
get over the fact the Son of God loved him and gave himself
for him. Peter was the same. He lived with a heart full of living
hope because of past grace, present grace and future grace.
Sometimes we can become so absorbed with petty problems
and problem people that we lose this grateful heart. We
become irritable and contemptible. We live with a short fuse
and it is no surprise when a few relational fireworks are set

off. Friendships are damaged, fellowship is marred and we create unnecessary difficulties for both ourselves and others. The root cause has been an ungrateful heart. A superficial platitude has replaced substantial gratitude. Words have become empty and hurtful. Graceless attitudes have kicked in and grace-filled attitudes have been kicked out. There is an urgent need in the world today for people to know what we in the church are for, rather than hearing too often what we are against. Christian trailblazers are people who are so thankful to God that they pour out their lives in loving, devoted service. They make a difference. They help people, and love the loveless. They birth initiatives, and put to death unfair practices. They oppose injustice. They are a pleasure to work for and to work with.

Have we lost something of this grateful heart? Is it time to think again and start again? Have grumps and grumbles become a pattern of life rather than occasional blips? God's call is to gratitude. Again and again I have seen lives transformed and relationships revolutionized because of someone who is motivated by gratitude. It is their dominant attitude and it has changed their life. John Newton the slave trader became John Newton the slave releaser, and author of the hymn *Amazing Grace*, because of his profound gratitude for God's undeserved grace. This was the turning point of his life. His selfishness was smashed. His old life crashed. A new life was born . . . and all because of God's amazing grace. Peter could have written that famous hymn. He too had known amazing grace and so he became a grateful man. True gratitude is expressed in real generosity. This is the third G.

Generosity

A Yorkshire man gave me a definition of a Yorkshire man – so please note the source! He said that a Yorkshire man was a

Scots man with the generosity squeezed out of him. I cannot comment, but I can say without fear of contradiction that one of the expressions of gratitude is generosity. How many people overstretch themselves in generous gifts and acts of kindness because they are deeply grateful? As we read Peter's epistles, we read the thoughts of a generous man. He promotes a generosity of spirit in our relationship with God, with others, with those we live with and with those we work with. This generosity of spirit is also to be extended towards those who oppose, criticize and insult us.

> Finally, all of you, have unity of spirit, sympathy, brotherly love, a tender heart, and a humble mind. Do not repay evil for evil or reviling for reviling, but on the contrary, bless, for to this you were called, that you may obtain a blessing.
> (1 Peter 3:8–9, English Standard Version)

Peter has witnessed this calling being worked out in someone's life. He has seen this generous love and loving generosity in Jesus. In his own heart, he knows about bounteous forgiveness. He cannot forget the cross. He is working out in life the words he was taught to pray: 'Forgive us our debts, as we also have forgiven our debtors' (Matthew 6:12). He knows that Jesus himself prayed for those who reviled him: 'Father, forgive them, for they do not know what they are doing' (Luke 23:34). Now Peter teaches what he has seen practised.

It is this kind of Christ-like generosity which makes such an impact in the minds and hearts of people accustomed to living for themselves. In *The Message*, Eugene Peterson paraphrases Peter in this way:

> Summing up: Be agreeable, be sympathetic, be loving, be compassionate, be humble. That goes for all of you, no

exceptions. No retaliation. No sharp-tongued sarcasm. Instead, bless – that's your job, to bless. You'll be a blessing and also get a blessing.

> Whoever wants to embrace life
>   and see the day fill up with good,
> Here's what you do:
>   Say nothing evil or hurtful;
> Snub evil and cultivate good;
>   run after peace for all you're worth.
> God looks on all this with approval,
>   listening and responding well to what he's asked;
> But he turns his back
>   on those who do evil things.
> (1 Peter 3:8–12, *The Message*)

People today are tired of words and need to see generous deeds and acts of kindness. The church cannot preach good news and in the community be bad news. Recently I preached in a church which gives over ninety per cent of its annual income to mission. After the tsunami in 2004, this church sent a love gift to a missionary family working and living in an area which had been badly affected by the disaster. The gift was sent with the following instructions. The sum of money was to pay for three fishing boats for fishermen who had lost their boats in the disaster. Two were to be given to Christian fishermen and one to a non-Christian. The instructions were carried out to the letter. All three recipients were stunned at such generosity, not least the fisherman who wasn't a Christian. On his first day out fishing with his brand-new boat, he caught a fish which was so big it was the equivalent of a month's catch. His response was, 'There must be a God!' He came to faith. An act of generosity in a church on one side of the world resulted in an experience of grace and a changed life in another part of the world.

When Christians are stingy and mean but claim to worship a God of generous grace, there is a contradiction between faith and works. Biblically, faith and works are inextricably linked. From the past we can look at the impact of someone like General William Booth, the founder of the Salvation Army. His was a ministry of generous care and practical support. Millions of lives have been influenced through the Salvation Army. In the present we can look at the ministry of generous acts of kindness through people like Jackie Pullinger and her team. They minister among the poor and the drug addicts of Hong Kong. As we look back at Peter's life, we see the impact of the healing of a man through him and John. Their ministry led to a miracle right beside a building set apart for God . . . We'll look at this in the next chapter of this book.

But what is the next chapter in your life? Will it be growth in grace? Will you be a more thankful, grateful person? Will your life be marked by generosity? Will the local church of which you are a member be known in the community as a group of generous, thoughtful, caring, big-hearted people? Are we, and will we be, 3G leaders and 3G churches? I am fully convinced that where there is a genuine commitment to these 3Gs, we will see changed lives and kingdom growth. It will take time, but it will come because this is the church as Jesus called it to be. He himself was the first 3G leader. He was full of grace and truth. He lived with an attitude of gratitude. He was, and is, overflowing in his expression of unmerited and undeserved generosity.

Ponder

1. In which areas of life do you need to take action so that you are more grace-filled and generous, in both words and actions?
2. Do you often express gratitude?
3. In your attitudes towards other people, are you generous or mean? Is there anyone to whom you need to apologize?
4. How could you grow in generosity in your regular financial giving?

Prayer

Lord, thank you for those who have shown me generosity. Forgive me for the times I have been mean-spirited and hard-hearted. Forgive us in the church for the hurt we have caused others. Have mercy on us. Lord, I commit myself to being a 3G Christian and leader. I also commit myself to encourage others to be 3G disciples. Lord, thank you for all the grace and generosity I have found in you. Amen.

13. Peter's ABC . . . humility, not celebrity

If any events illustrate the power of God to change a life and transform a character, they are those described in Acts 2 – 4. Peter preaches to thousands. He doesn't deny Christ. He declares Christ. He prays for healing. He is arrested because of his brave witness. We see a Peter who is courageous, not diffident.

> When they saw the courage of Peter and John and realized
> that they were unschooled, ordinary men, they were
> astonished and they took note that these men had been
> with Jesus.
> (Acts 4:13)

Peter is humble, not arrogant. He is dependent on Christ, not focused on himself. He has grown so much both in faith and in humility. In Acts 3 we read of Peter and John together in their discipleship and devotions. It is the afternoon and they are going to pray. They have been filled with the Holy Spirit on the day of Pentecost. They have embarked on apostolic ministry. They are on a new mission, carrying out kingdom work and outreach. These are heady days. Little do they know what is just about to happen in the temple precincts.

However, there is an important principle which opened the door to an amazing miracle. This is often overlooked. Despite all that has happened, and all the blessings Peter and John have experienced, they have not jettisoned basic disciplines of training and discipleship which nourish growth. They still have fixed points in their lives which strengthen and deepen their relationship with the God they love so much. These fixed points open doors of usefulness and blessing.

Develop or ditch?

Some Christian leaders naively think that because they have been on the discipleship trail for a long time, they can ditch certain essential devotional disciplines. The reality is that we can't. These very practices have actually been lifelines. They have been essential ingredients of the backbone of our training in godliness. We miss them most when they are absent for a sustained length of time. It is easy to dismiss their importance and therefore downgrade their practice. Of course we do not make a false idol of any devotional practice, but neither do we assume a spiritual arrogance which suggests that, while others need such disciplines, we certainly don't. Surely the wiser approach is to develop our personal devotional life rather than jettison it.

Some Christians have given up meeting regularly with others in worship because of past hurts, deep disappointment or some other reason. They have no doubt about their love for Jesus. They just have given up meeting with his followers on a regular basis. Others have gone further and have decided that corporate worship, personal prayer and Bible study are now things of the past. Peter and John thought differently.

It is my experience that so often God speaks into my life in the ABCs of Christian living. As we do what he calls us to do, we receive fresh insights, creative ideas and refreshing thoughts. He speaks a word which we need to hear just at that particular time. It may be during a time of worship, when in a reading, a hymn, song, prayer or sermon, God speaks a word right into my heart and life. As a preacher I have found at different times the seeds of a sermon will come through my personal devotions, or as I am stirring in the morning or am awake at some stage in the night.

Some years ago when I was in Uganda to preach at the Nebbi Diocesan Convention I was invited to visit a mountain which had just been purchased by the Diocese (as you do!). It was to be a 'Prayer Mountain' to which groups, churches and individuals would go, specifically to pray. To my mind it was in the middle of nowhere. From near the summit one looked over to the Congo. When we arrived the Bishop said to me, 'See you in a few hours, I am going off to pray.' I found myself alone on the top of a mountain in this remote place in north-west Uganda and I can tell you, I prayed! The intensity of my prayer was fuelled by initial thoughts of armed Congolese rebels, heartless killers in the Lord's Resistance Army, indescribably dangerous wild animals and poisonous snakes. I anticipated all of these and more! No doubt these were irrational fears. To my shame I couldn't remember the last time I had set aside some hours to be alone with the Lord. That mountain became a special place, like the Mountain of Transfiguration was for Peter. Thankfully the Bishop remembered to collect me and when he did, I came away from that remote location, which was a 'Bethel' for me, with a renewed sense of God's call on my life. Through praying, praising, interceding and reading the Bible (which was all I had with me), I knew God had spoken something into my life. It was the following.

> The Sovereign LORD has given me a well-instructed tongue,
>> to know the word that sustains the weary.
> He wakens me morning by morning,
>> wakens my ear to listen like one being instructed.
> (Isaiah 50:4)

This text is also inscribed inside my bishop's ring, for those words have become pivotal to me in my understanding of God's call on my life. I would have missed them, had I thought I was beyond the basics of reading the Bible and praying. Look at what Peter and John would have missed, had they opted out of going to the temple at the hour of prayer . . . an astonishing incident, an amazing miracle, a dramatic healing. Their devotional discipline became the context of a life-changing encounter. The story begins with Acts 3:1–5 . . .

Dramatic happenings at Beautiful Gate

> One day Peter and John were going up to the temple at the time of prayer – at three in the afternoon. Now a man who was lame from birth was being carried to the temple gate called Beautiful, where he was put every day to beg from those going into the temple courts. When he saw Peter and John about to enter, he asked them for money. Peter looked straight at him, as did John. Then Peter said, 'Look at us!' So the man gave them his attention, expecting to get something from them.
> (Acts 3:1–5)

It is important to remember that this man had been crippled from birth. He had been like this for over forty years. He was utterly helpless and totally dependent on others. He couldn't walk and so most days he was carried to this particular place outside the temple. Undoubtedly he would have preferred a beautiful life rather than having to resort to begging outside the Beautiful Gate. What an existence, day after day. How demeaning, how demanding and how degrading. The Nicanor Gate (which the Beautiful Gate is widely believed to be) where the man was positioned was the main eastern entrance to the temple precincts. The double doors were huge and impressive and probably at least seventy-five feet high. He must have looked such a pathetic figure beside such grandeur. He asked Peter and John for money, just as he did of most passers-by. Luke, the writer of the Acts of the Apostles, tells us that Peter said to the man, 'Look at us!' (I wonder where Peter had learned the importance and value of the look.) Too often this man had looked up and found nothing. For years he was accustomed and resigned to looking at feet and legs as he stayed seated on the ground. No doubt he had given up on looking up. However, this time he did give the two apostles his attention, although they were complete strangers to him.

> Then Peter said, 'Silver or gold I do not have, but what I do have I give you. In the name of Jesus Christ of Nazareth, walk.' Taking him by the right hand, he helped him up, and instantly the man's feet and ankles became strong. He jumped to his feet and began to walk. Then he went with them into the temple courts, walking and jumping, and praising God. When all the people saw him walking and praising God, they recognized him as the same man who used to sit begging at the temple gate called Beautiful, and they were filled with wonder and amazement at what had happened to him.
> (Acts 3:6–10)

In the name of Jesus Christ of Nazareth, Peter commanded this man to walk . . . and he walked, leapt and praised God! As Peter had watched what Jesus did with the daughter of

Jairus, so he now did with the beggar at the gate. He took him by the hand and he helped him up. In his own family, Peter had watched Jesus take the hand of his ill mother-in-law and as Jesus helped her up, she was healed. This time it was Peter's hand that took a person's hand, but it was the same Lord's hand that touched his body. It was the power of Christ invading lifeless limbs. It was a dramatic miracle. The man was healed. He did not remain silent – by that afternoon, everyone in the temple knew about it. His was a familiar face, his plight a daily spectacle. Now there was a spectacle of a different kind, because the power of God had been released in motionless feet and powerless ankles. People had something to talk about that day when they went home from the temple. The man who was healed had even more. It was a powerful encounter of a divine kind.

Within moments of the healing, crowds had gathered. Peter seized the opportunity both to explain and to proclaim. This was a gospel moment. It was a kingdom encounter. People had seen the deeds and now they heard the words.

> While the man held on to Peter and John, all the people were astonished and came running to them in the place called Solomon's Colonnade. When Peter saw this, he said to them: 'Fellow Israelites, why does this surprise you? Why do you stare at us as if by our own power or godliness we had made this man walk? The God of Abraham, Isaac and Jacob, the God of our fathers, has glorified his servant Jesus. You handed him over to be killed, and you disowned him before Pilate, though he had decided to let him go. You disowned the Holy and Righteous One and asked that a murderer be released to you. You killed the author of life, but God raised him from the dead. We are witnesses of this. By faith in the name of Jesus, this man whom you see and know was made strong. It is Jesus'

name and the faith that comes through him that has
completely healed him, as you can all see.'
(Acts 3:11–16)

Hearing with their eyes

People today hear with their eyes. When they see the Christian
faith, the power, truth and love of God being lived out in
practical generous ways, they take notice. They ask questions,
and listen more intently. The church is called to care both in
proclaiming the word and doing the deeds. This is the Jesus
way . . . proclamation and demonstration. God still cares for
hurting, lonely, sick people. His power is still the same. His love
is still as deep. Through the compassion and courage of a
faithful Peter, God's power is released into people's lives and it
is the same today. When we in the church exercise a leadership
which is one of utter dependence on God, Christ-exalting and
self-denying, then it is amazing what God will do. On our
wedding day we sang the following hymn by Kate Wilkinson.
The words could have been written by Peter. Each verse encap-
sulates some of the traits of his life and priorities so evident in
this event. All the focus is on Jesus. Peter draws no attention
to himself. He preaches Christ. He exalts Christ. He ministers
in the name of Christ. These words are worth digesting.

May the mind of Christ, my Saviour,
Live in me from day to day,
By His love and power controlling
All I do and say.

May the Word of God dwell richly
In my heart from hour to hour,
So that all may see I triumph
Only through His power.

May the peace of God my Father
Rule my life in everything,
That I may be calm to comfort
Sick and sorrowing.

May the love of Jesus fill me
As the waters fill the sea;
Him exalting, self abasing,
This is victory.

May I run the race before me,
Strong and brave to face the foe,
Looking only unto Jesus
As I onward go.

May His beauty rest upon me,
As I seek the lost to win,
And may they forget the channel,
Seeing only Him.

Our forgotten identity

In subtle ways, even in Christian leadership, we can become
self-driven, self-focused and self-absorbed, despite our claims
to be the opposite. We see ourselves primarily as leaders and
God's gift to the church, rather than understanding that we
are his channels and children. Our principal identity is not that
of leader but as a son or daughter of the living God. We may
be making disciples, but we are still disciples ourselves and we
are disciples before we are leaders. Sometimes we forget that.
Some of us have become intoxicated with power and praise.
These feed our egos, but suffocate our souls. We have bowed
down to the idol of influence. Humility flies out the door. In
a situation like Peter and John's, we take the credit to ourselves.

They didn't! We have stolen what is for God's glory alone. Our most-sung worship song is 'I will lift *my* name on high'. We are on highly dangerous ground; indeed, we are walking in a ministry minefield and at any moment we may implode or explode.

Perhaps we have fallen into the mindset where an invitation is accepted on the basis of financial reward. A prayer is prayed, but we have already decided the outcome. A pastoral situation is addressed in order to meet our own needs. A statement is given so that we are made to look good. A friendship is fostered for selfish benefit. A sermon is preached, but it is really to get at someone. We need to learn from Peter, because all of these traits are echoes of the immature Peter. How different Peter is now. Self-glory is taboo. He is a mixture and model of Christ-centred creeds and Christ-glorifying deeds. He practises what he preaches. He speaks of repentance and he has repented. A golden rule is that we too need to practise what we preach.

The humble leader

I will never forget being asked to be the chairman at a large public meeting in Dublin. The Reverend Dr John Stott was the speaker. I met him thirty-five minutes before the meeting and then showed him to a room where he could be quiet. He asked me to come for him about ten minutes before the meeting. I did. I knocked on the door and heard the words, 'Come in, brother.' I will never forget the sight I saw. Here was this gifted preacher and teacher, this author of many books, this world-famous Christian leader, kneeling before a chair on which his Bible was open and his notes were beside him. He said, 'Brother, pray with me.' I don't remember one word I prayed. I just know I did. For me, his was an example of utter humility before God in the presence of a very young and inexperienced leader. He had probably given this lecture many times before, but he needed to pray. There was no arrogant hierarchical leadership mindset which prevented him asking for prayer. Like Peter, his holiness was evidenced in humility. Like Peter, repentance and dependence, not celebrity reputation and extravagant lifestyle, were the realities and priorities in his life.

> Now, fellow Israelites, I know that you acted in ignorance, as did your leaders. But this is how God fulfilled what he had foretold through all the prophets, saying that his Messiah would suffer. Repent, then, and turn to God, so that your sins may be wiped out, that times of refreshing may come from the Lord, and that he may send the Messiah, who has been appointed for you – even Jesus.
> (Acts 3:17–20)

Peter knows all about the times of refreshing, for he has tasted them himself. He has been refreshed. He has turned his back on his selfish living. In the past, he was a drain on people. He was arrogant, boisterous and wearisome, but now he is a refreshing person to be with . . . just like Jesus. Is this a quality you need to recapture? How do others find you? Are you tiresome and demanding in an offensive way? Are you insensitive as Peter used to be? You may not feel stressed, but you may carry stress which is passed on to others. It is time to change.

In Acts 2 – 4, we see a Peter who has changed. He is humble and holy. He is courageous and compassionate. He is living a life worthy of his calling – we are called to the same.

Ponder

1. Have you shifted from a Christ-like servant leadership model to a celebrity status model of ministry? Do you ever find yourself, in subtle ways, feeding your ego or are you living for Christ?
2. Would it be helpful to talk with someone about your devotional disciplines – and which areas in particular?

Prayer

Forgive me, Lord, that in my insecurity and arrogance, I sometimes move away from the Jesus way. Lord, I am determined to reject all that is unworthy of you. Fill me with your Holy Spirit that I may be humble, holy and wholesome. Amen.

Postscript

I have always been fascinated by the following life story, of someone in the USA.

As a child, this man was forced out of his home with his family when he was seven years old. When he was only nine, and a backward, shy little boy, his mother died. As a store clerk at twenty-two, he lost his job. He wanted to go to law school but his education was not good enough. At twenty-three he went into debt to become a partner in a small store. Three years later his business partner died, leaving him a huge debt that took years to repay. A romance ended in heartache because the young lady died. At twenty-eight, after four years of developing a romantic relationship with another young lady, she rejected his proposal of marriage.

He tried to enter politics, but twice failed to be elected to Congress. At thirty-seven, on his third try, he was finally successful. Two years later, he ran again, but this time failed to be re-elected and at this time had what some would call a nervous breakdown. At forty-one, being now somewhat unhappily married, he experienced the additional heartache of his four-year-old son's death. At forty-five, he ran for the Senate and lost. At forty-nine, he ran for the Senate again and lost. On top of all this, he faced constant criticism, misunderstanding, ugly and false rumours, and deep periods of depression. However, at fifty-one, he was elected President of the United States. He became the most inspirational and highly regarded President in American history.

Who was he? Abraham Lincoln.

Failure after failure . . . yet he kept going and made decisive positive choices.

Peter did the same. He had many failures, disappointments and setbacks, but by the grace of God he kept going . . . and look at the result. The story of Peter is a good news story. It is a story of hope. God can do the same for you and me.

One famous actor, Oscar-winning Ben Affleck, who has faced many personal battles, was interviewed by Louise Gannon. She entitled the article 'Failure was the making of me' and quoted Ben Affleck as saying . . .

> I think we all make mistakes – it is all about how you deal with them. I've been very, very hot and very, very cold . . . There's a lot to be said about how you face adversity, how you react – and how you move on.

Certainly with Peter it was out of failure that a great leader emerged. By the grace of God he moved on. He became a faithful disciple. He opened his life unreservedly to Christ. He was willing to learn. He faced his prejudices. His focus was clear, and his potential was realized. His gifts were unleashed. He was committed to keeping on persevering.

In the making of many great leaders, the path to maturity is one of obstacles and struggles. How we react to them and in them is a key to growth. Peter's Lord discipled him. Peter's God gave the growth. Whatever your circumstances, whatever your situation, no matter how serious your failures and how deep your disappointments, he is 'the God of all grace, who . . . will himself restore you and make you strong, firm and steadfast. To him be the power for ever and ever. Amen' (1 Peter 5:10–11).

Notes

Chapter 5: Listen to him . . . focus on him
1. James S. Kunen, 'It Ain't Us, Babe', *Time* magazine, 1 September 1997.
2. E. Stanley Ott, *Transform Your Church with Ministry Teams* (Eerdmans, Grand Rapids, 2004).

Chapter 9: Do you love me?
1. *In The Name of Jesus* (Darton Longman and Todd, London, 1989).

Chapter 10: Pride and prejudice
1. From 'What Ten Years Have Taught Me', *Christian Century*, 17 February 1960. Used with permission.

Chapter 11: The priority of obedience
1. *Jesus Among Other Gods* (Thomas Nelson Inc., Nashville, Tennessee, 2001), reprinted by permission. All rights reserved.

For more information about IVP
and our publications visit
www.ivpbooks.com

Get regular updates at **ivpbooks.com/signup**
Find us on **facebook.com/ivpbooks**
Follow us on **twitter.com/ivpbookcentre**

Inter-Varsity Press, a company limited by guarantee registered in England and Wales, number 05202650. Registered
office IVP Bookcentre, Norton Street, Nottingham NG7 3HR, United Kingdom. Registered charity number 1105757.